A Journey through Southern Arizona

Victoria Clark

Schiffer® Publishing Ltd
4880 Lower Valley Road, Atglen, Pennsylvania 19310

Other Schiffer Books by Victoria Clark

A Journey through Northern Arizona
978-0-7643-3010-0, $24.99

Other Schiffer Books on Related Subjects:

Touring the West with the Fred Harvey & Co. and the Santa Fe Railway
978-0-7643-3110-7, $24.99

Tucson's Most Haunted,
978-0-7643-3153-4, $14.99

Scare-Izona: A Guide to Arizona's Legendary Haunts,
978-0-7643-2844-2, $14.95

Santa Fe & Surrounds
0-7643-2301-6, $24.95

Library of Congress Control Number: 2009925167

Designed by Stephanie Daugherty
Type set in Adobe Jenson Pro/Souvenir Lt BT/Humanst521 BT

ISBN: 978-0-7643-3269-2
Printed in China

Schiffer Books are available at special discounts for bulk purchases for sales promotions or premiums. Special editions, including personalized covers, corporate imprints, and excerpts can be created in large quantities for special needs. For more information contact the publisher:

Published by Schiffer Publishing Ltd.
4880 Lower Valley Road
Atglen, PA 19310
Phone: (610) 593-1777; Fax: (610) 593-2002
E-mail: Info@schifferbooks.com

For the largest selection of fine reference books on this and related subjects, please visit our web site at **www.schifferbooks.com.**

We are always looking for people to write books on new and related subjects. If you have an idea for a book please contact us at the above address.

This book may be purchased from the publisher. Include $5.00 for shipping. Please try your bookstore first. You may write for a free catalog.

In Europe, Schiffer books are distributed by
Bushwood Books
6 Marksbury Ave.
Kew Gardens
Surrey TW9 4JF England
Phone: 44 (0) 20 8392 8585; Fax: 44 (0) 20 8392 9876
E-mail: info@bushwoodbooks.co.uk
Website: www.bushwoodbooks.co.uk

Contents

Preface

My parents, Jacque and Glenn Schoder, spent time working in Tucson, Arizona, during World War ll. By 1951, they moved back to Tucson and purchased a tiny adobe house not far from the University of Arizona. While the house was tiny, the yard was well established with grass, flowers, palms, and citrus trees. The walled backyard patio was our outdoor living room. Our visiting family was always thrilled to pick oranges, grapefruit, and lemons from the trees in our yard during the winter months. Most of our guests never imagined that so many trees and flowers grew in Southern Arizona. Visitors usually wanted to hike in the Sabino Canyon, picnic on Mount Lemmon, stroll through the movie sets at Old Tucson, visit the San Xavier Mission, shop for curios in downtown Tucson, and buy leather goods and zarapes in Nogales, Mexico. All of our visitors wanted a chance to sit in the sunshine and write postcards to family and friends "back home" about Arizona's weather. Thank goodness so many visitors sent those wonderful postcards—many of which have survived—and I'm often amused with their jottings about Arizona.

On Vacation. My parents, Jacque and Glenn Schoder, and friend Edith Remus at the Swan Road Riding Stable in Tucson, Arizona, *1945*.

It was my good fortune to grow up in Tucson, and I have always been grateful for the multicultural neighborhood that I grew up in. The days were sunny with blue skies, the sunsets vivid, and the night skies were bright with glittering stars. My parents should have worked for Tucson's Chamber of Commerce because eventually other members of our family moved to Arizona. As an adult, I have lived in central and northern Arizona, which have their own unique beauty, but I have to admit that there isn't anything that smells quite as good to me as the scent of the creosote bushes in the Sonoran Desert after a summer rain.

Introduction

In 1539, Spanish Conquistadors entered the area that would become the state of Arizona to search for gold. They didn't find the cities lined with gold that they sought, but they did explore, map, and establish small communities and missions, which paved the way for others to arrive. During the years that followed, present day Arizona would belong to Spain and then Mexico until Mexico was forced to cede the area to the United States following the Mexican-American War. The remainder of present day Arizona was purchased by the United States as a part of the Gadsden Purchase. Arizona became a U.S. Territory in 1863 and was admitted into statehood as the forty-eighth state in 1912.

Southern Arizona is an area of great diversity with its vast Sonoran Desert, pine covered rugged mountain ranges, and lush riparian areas. Mining and ranching fueled its early growth, and later, citrus, date, and farming became important to Southern Arizona's economy. Those who sought the health benefits of sunshine and dry air began arriving in Arizona in significant numbers. Little did the Spanish Conquistadors realize that they had found pure gold in the form of the sunshine that would create Arizona's lasting tourist industry.

Section 1: Tourist Funnies

When word spread that reliable train service and first-rate lodging was available in Arizona—the land of dry air, sunshine, and fantastic landscapes—tourists began arriving. And they have kept arriving ever since. Tourists today are very savvy, as there are a number of great travel guides and websites to peruse for virtual tours of the areas they wish to visit, but Arizona's early tourists expected that Arizona would look just like their favorite Western films. No wonder enterprising artists and postcard publishers made a good living by capturing this treasure trove of humor.

Chapter One:

The Artists

Hal Empie

Hart "Hal" Empie (1909-2002) was born in a one-room adobe ranch house near Safford, Arizona. As a boy, Hal was enterprising and sold a variety of products. His good reputation earned him a job in a drug store, which led Hal to enroll at the University of Arizona in a medical program. When he graduated at the age of 20, Hal was Arizona's youngest licensed pharmacist. He found work as a pharmacist and also opened a sign painting business. Hal and his wife, Louise, moved to Duncan, Arizona in 1934 to manage the Duncan Drug Store, and by 1937, he bought the drugstore.

Though working as a pharmacist, Hal also wanted to show his paintings, so he renamed the drug store the Art Gallery Drug Store and displayed his paintings on the walls. Tourists usually wanted postcards, and Hal saw an opportunity to create humorous Western cartoon postcards. He named his postcards, Empie Kartoon Kards, and sold them for five cents each. Soon orders for Empie Kartoon Kards were placed by other drug stores, and some of his postcards were published in newspapers and magazines. Hal would eventually move to Tubac, Arizona, where he opened the Hal Empie Studio & Gallery and sold his sketches and fine art paintings.

Greetings from Southern Arizona. "Hello—Had a Hard Trip—I'm In No Shape to Talk." Empie Kartoon Kards, Duncan, Arizona, *1946*, *$6-8*.

An Empire Card. Way Out West. "About Have Things Under Control. Will Write If Nothing Happens." Empie Kartoon Kards, Duncan, Arizona, *1939*, *$6-8*.

Way Out West. Trying to Take It Easy on this Trip. Empie Kartoon Kards, Duncan, Arizona, *circa 1940s, $6-8.*

Way Out West. "Paleface Better Gettum Hoss." Hal Empie, *copyright 1936, $6-8.*

Greetings from Th' Grand Canyon. Under Th' Circumstances I Couldn't Think of Writing A Letter. Empie Kartoon Kards, *1938, $8-10.*

Out West in Th' Cactus Country. "Lookit, Wilbur—They're Flat!" Empie Kartoon Kards, Duncan, Arizona, *copyright 1948, $6-8.*

Howdy from the Land of the Giant Cactus. Reg Manning Travelcard No.12, C.T. Art Colortone, *1942, $4-6.*

Reg Manning

Reginald (Reg) Manning (1905-1986) came from Kansas City, Missouri to Phoenix, Arizona as a boy in 1919. Those who knew Reg said that he sketched everything that interested him. Reg attended Phoenix Union High School, where he formed a lasting friendship with Barry Goldwater and met his future wife, Ruth. After graduating near the top of his class, Reg rented space at a small printing company and worked as a commercial illustrator and cartoonist. In 1924, he was hired by Gov. George W. P. Hunt to draw political campaign cartoons. He joined the staff of *The Arizona Republican* (now *The Arizona Republic*) in 1927 for the salary of $175 per month. While his primary duty was staff photographer, he published a cartoon page titled "The Big Parade" that featured his scantily-clad cowgirl named Lil Dudette. Reg's cartoons and humorous editorials about politicians became extremely popular. His editorial cartoons were published not only in *The Arizona Republic,* but 170 other newspapers across America and around the world. In 1944, Reg's first book, *Little Itchy Itchy,* which featured World War II cartoons, sold 10,000 copies. His political cartoon titled, "Hats," which depicted silk top hats and a soldier's helmet with a bullet hole in it on top of a cross in Korea, won him the Pulitzer Prize in 1951 and a listing in *Who's Who in the World*. Reg's talent as a fine artist led him to produce jewelry, watercolors, fabrics, greeting cards, postcards, and engravings on fine crystal.

Desert Desperados. Reg Manning Travelcard No. 3, C.T. Art Colortone, *1941, $6-8.*

Beauties of the Far West. The sexy cowgirl is Reg Manning's "Big Parade Comic Strip" character Lil Dudette. Travelcard No. 36, C.T. Art Colortone, *1948, $10-12.*

"The Southwest Is Well Guarded from Parachutists." A Reg Manning Travelcard No. 9-41, C.T. Art Colortone, *1941, $6-8.*

The Famous Laughing Cactus.
This Desert Air is so Penetrating—
It Pierces to the Depth of Your Being.
Reg Manning Travelcard No.4-41. C.T. Art Colortone, *1941, $6-8.*

Wild West Golf: Two Shots Then Drive to the Hole on Boot Hill.
A Reg Manning Travelcard No. 8-41, C.T. Art Colortone, *1941, $6-8.*

Bob Petley

Bob Teeple Petley (1912-2006) was born in Akron, Ohio. He attended West High School in Akron and the Culver Military Academy, where he competed and honed his boxing skills. He won a regional Golden Gloves title in 1931, and attended Hiram College in Ohio. From 1937 to 1943, Bob sold candy for the Life Saver Company. Problems with arthritis prompted Bob and his family to move to Phoenix, Arizona where Bob worked for *The Arizona Republic* and the *Phoenix Gazette* selling display advertising. Bob recognized the potential of the tourist industry in Arizona. He drew twelve humorous black and white postcards related to tourists in the desert, which he began selling from wooden racks decorated with rope. Before long, his "side" job of creating postcards became his full time job. Bob continued to draw and market his comic Laff Cards, but he also could literally be found all over the West, taking color photos from the top of his van. The photos were published by his publishing company, Petley Studios, and at one time, Petley Studios was America's largest publisher of scenic color postcards with sales of over twenty-five million postcards annually.

"The Trip's Been Uneventful..So Far." Petley, No. 1, the Cowboy Cartoonist, Phoenix, Arizona, *1945, $6-8.*

Western Hospitality. Petley No. 5, the Cowboy Cartoonist, Phoenix, Arizona, *1945, $6-8.*

Greetings from the Romantic West. Petley No. 7, the Cowboy Cartoonist, Phoenix, Arizona, *1945, $6-8.*

A Petley Card. Havin' A Wonderful Time and Ahm' Sure Not Takin Any Chances. Bob Petley Laff Card C-27, Phoenix, Arizona, *1952, $6-8.*

Humor Card. Look, Dearie At the Friendly Little Snake...He's Waggin' His Tail At Me! Bob Petley Laff Card C-30, *1955, $6-8.*

Justa Pausin' Fer A Little Refreshin.' Bob Petley Laff Card C-49, *circa 1957, $6-8.*

Section Two: Plants and Animals of the Sonoran Desert

A Smoke Tree on the Desert. Smoke trees grow in sandy areas along the washes. If a seed with its tough outer layer isn't opened, then the seed isn't able to reproduce, but if the seed is carried along the wash too far, then the seed is smashed apart and dies. A delicate balance of nature is required. C.T. Art Colortone, *circa 1940s, $4-6.*

Chapter Two:

Cacti and Trees

Since some people envision a desert as miles of rock and sand dunes, they are surprised to discover the diversity of the cacti, flowers, plants, trees, animals, birds, insects, and reptiles that thrive in the Sonoran Desert. Arizona has the largest portion of the Sonoran Desert in the United States, which extends up from Mexico on either side of the Gulf of California. The landscape is characterized by canyons and mountains, and washes with sandy beds and low banks that can carry surprising amounts of water after a significant rainfall, but it's the saguaro cactus that is the definitive symbol of the Sonoran Desert.

The plants and animals in the Sonoran Desert have undergone amazing adaptations to survive in the harsh climate, as summer temperatures can reach as high of 120 degrees. During the months of spring, if rains have been plentiful, the desert becomes a carpet of wildflowers. If rainfall has been scarce, wildflower seeds can remain dormant but viable for many seasons.

There are laws against removal of desert plants, animals, and reptiles that impose fines and even jail time, but thieves and vandals continue to rob the desert of its diversity. Even the well intentioned who feed wildlife upset nature's balance, and those who try to keep desert animals or reptiles as pets rob them of the chance to reproduce. Fortunately there are also naturalist groups that offer education, publications, and conservation projects that help people to appreciate the Sonoran Desert for its unique ecosystem.

There is an enormous variety of plants, animals, birds, and creepy critters in the Sonoran Desert that were not widely photographed and published by early postcard companies, if they photographed the desert at all. For example, common creosote bushes, various types of sagebrush, and mesquite trees weren't deemed worthy by photographers who favored photos of unusual forms of cacti. Most of the early photographers were focused on capturing images of people, buildings, and events of the time. Since many of the animals of the Sonoran Desert have adapted to the blistering heat by foraging at night, or moving at extreme speeds, early photographers did not have the sophisticated equipment necessary to capture their images.

The Joshua Palm. The Joshua Palm is a native of the desert in Southern Arizona. The trunk of a Joshua resembles a tree; however, Joshuas are members of the lily family. Joshua Trees are able to survive in the most arid areas of the desert because their leaves have a tremendous capacity to store water. A.O. Boeres Company, Phoenix, Arizona, *1928, $6-8.*

Yucca Palms in the Desert, Arizona. Also known as Joshua Palms or Joshua Trees, Yucca Palms have surrealistic forms and can grow to a height of over thirty feet. A.O. Boeres Company, Phoenix, Arizona, *1928, $6-8.*

Strawberry or Hedgehog Cactus. The hedgehog cactus grows in clumps of four to eight arms. Buds form at the ends of the arms and produce showy red purple blooms usually during the month of April. C.T. Art Colortone, *circa 1940s, $4-6.*

Organ Pipe Cacti. The Organ Pipe can be found growing in rocky soils in the lower regions of the Sonoran Desert. The stems, called pipes, grow from a central trunk, and at a distance, they appear as large bushes. Under favorable conditions, an organ pipe cactus can live over one hundred years. The Organ Pipe National Monument, located on 300,000 acres of desert land just south of Ajo, was established in 1937. C.T. Art Colortone, *circa 1940s, $4-6.*

Ocotillo Cactus. With showy orange-red blooms that appear at the ends of the stalks, the Ocotillo was sometimes called Coach Whip because of its tall whip-like stalks that can grow to heights of twelve feet. The stalks are joined at a single base. The Ocotillo can shed and grow its leaves up to six times a year depending on the amount of rainfall. When planted in a row, the Ocotillo makes an effective fence. C.T. Art Colortone, *circa 1940s, $4-6.*

A Pincushion Cactus, the Flower of the Desert. The name Pincushion cactus actually refers to a group of over 175 different varieties of small cacti that can grow to about six inches in height and have a small round shape with reddish hooked spines. The flowers appear in early spring, which are pollinated by bees, and the tiny fruits are enjoyed by the birds and rodents. There are ten varieties of Pincushion cacti that grow in Arizona. C.T. Photochrome, *1910, $6-8.*

Cacti

Barrel

The barrel cactus was named for its round shape, and its "pleats" store water within their spongy tissues. The barrel expands during rainfall and shrinks as it utilizes the stored water. The roots are shallow but extensive, sometimes growing just inches below the ground, and the barrel can survive on a minimum of rainfall. A barrel cactus grows facing south to prevent its flesh from sunburn. During the summer, the barrel produces flowers that range from yellow to orange depending upon the variety of barrel, and its fruits form in miniature pineapple shapes. While the fruits lack the sweet fleshy pulp of many of the other cactus fruits, the fruits and seeds of the barrel cacti are eaten by birds and packrats. The spines of the barrel are flat with a hook shape on the ends and help to shade the cactus. A mature barrel can weigh over one hundred pounds.

Night Blooming Cereus

The Night Blooming Cereus appears as a dead gray green stick most of the year. In late May or early June, buds appear on the ends of the seemingly dead stalks. Only on one night a year will the blooms open, at which time they emit a strong spicy odor. The large blooms open at dusk and remain open until mid morning—just long enough to have attracted insects to pollinate the flowers. Once pollinated, the flowers produce bright red fruits that are eaten by the birds that deposit the seeds.

Barrel Cactus (Visnaga) on the Desert. Western Publishing & Novelty Co., *1948, $4-6.*

Night Blooming Cereus. C.T. Art Colortone, *circa 1940s, $5-6.*

Cholla

There are various types of cholla such as cane, staghorn, and teddy bear, which have viciously painful spines that resemble bee stings when encountered. Chollas grow in jointed segments that can break off easily when brushed against. Once broken off, the segment imbeds itself into the passerby and it is very difficult to remove. The spines protect the cholla against desert foragers, but also serve to block the intense sunlight. It seems unlikely, but the cholla is a favorite place for cactus wrens to build their nests. While chollas bloom between May and June and produce fruit, most chollas reproduce when their segments fall off and take root under favorable conditions.

Greetings from Arizona. A group of cholla cacti. Cholla have jointed, fine, fuzzy spines that break off so easily when they are brushed against that appear to "jump" on the unlucky passerby. RPPC, *circa 1950, $6-8.*

Cholla cactus.
C.T. Art Colortone,
circa 1940s, $4-6.

Prickly Pear

Prickly pear cactus pads (nopal) are stripped of their spines and cooked as nopalitos, which have been a food staple of Sonoran desert dwellers for centuries. Visitors to the Sonoran Desert are often shocked to see cattle munching on the spiny prickly pear pads. The substances found in the pads and fruit of the prickly pear are being studied as having the ability to lower blood sugar in diabetics and LDL or "bad" cholesterol. The bright red fruit are called pears and are harvested in August. Once the spines have been removed, the fruit is cooked, strained, and boiled into syrup. The syrup is used as a sweetener, for flavoring prickly pear margaritas and making jelly. The bright red juice of prickly pear fruit has been used for centuries as a dye.

Prickly Pear Cactus in Bloom. C.T. Art Colortone, *1944, $4-6.*

Prickly Pear. The prickly pear cactus blooms in April and May. The blossoms range in color from a light yellow to a flaming orange. C.T. Art Colortone, *circa 1940s, $4-6.*

Saguaro

The stately saguaro, traditionally spelled sahuaro, is a symbol of the state of Arizona, and the saguaro blossom is Arizona's official state flower. Saguaros are extremely slow growing and may only grow an inch or two in ten years. A saguaro will not grow an arm until it is approximately fifty years old. The tough waxy outer skin has rows of cross-pointed sharp spines to protect the cactus. Inside the saguaro is a skeleton of ribs; each rib is about two inches wide. For such a massive body, it would be reasonable to assume that a saguaro had a deep taproot, but the saguaro has a very shallow, but extensive, root system that allows it more flexibility to sway in strong winds. Crème colored flowers form at the tops of the saguaro's arms. The flowers do not all bloom at the same time, and each flower is only open for a few hours. The nectar of the saguaro is sucked by bats, white winged doves, moths, and honeybees that pollinate the flowers. When the waxy flowers die, the fruit begins to form. Each saguaro fruit is crimson colored, about the size of a fist, and has approximately 2,000 seeds. The fruits of the saguaro have been harvested for centuries by Native desert dwellers, who use ten to twenty feet long saguaro dried ribs as poles. Creosote branches are attached near the top of the poles to help loosen the fruit. The tough peel of the fruit is cut, or if the fruit is ripe enough, it splits open, revealing the sweet red pulp. The fruit is boiled and carefully strained. The gathering, cooking, and straining process takes hours, but the result is a sweet syrup that many people compare to molasses. In keeping with tradition, the peels and strained seeds are returned to the earth to be eaten by animals and birds. While historically the saguaro fruit had ceremonial purposes and was used as a sweetener, today it is primarily used to make jams.

Famous Walking Saguaro Cactus. Photo by R.C. Proctor, C.T. Art Colortone, *circa 1940s, $4-6.*

A rare-crested Saguaro Cactus. Sandoval News Company, *circa 1940s, $5-7.*

Giant Saguaro Cactus, sixty feet high. A saguaro can weigh up to two tons. (It was a common practice to photograph a saguaro with people or horses standing underneath to show the spectacular height of the saguaro.) *Circa 1915, $8-11.*

Blossoms of the Saguaro Giant Cactus, Arizona's State Flower. C.T. Art Colortone, *circa 1940s, $4-6.*

The "Watermellon Tree," a freak Saguaro Giant Cactus. C.T. Art Colortone Colored, *1947, $6-8.*

Saguaro Blossoms, Arizona's State Flower. C.T. Art Colortone, *circa 1940s, $4-6.*

Palo Verde Tree

The palo verde, meaning green stick in Spanish, is Arizona's state tree and it is easy for newcomers to the Sonoran Desert to identify, because of its green bark, green branches, and green leaves. In years of draught, the palo verde does not produce leaves. If the tree has produced leaves, it will shed them before it is time to bloom. At the end of spring, usually in May or early June, the palo verde produces showy yellow blossoms that appear at the ends of their branches. The flowers turn brown and produce seedpods that resemble yellow wax beans. While the palo verde produces many seeds, the number of seeds that become seedlings is relatively small. If seedlings grow during a year of little rainfall, they whither and die; also, they are often a favorite food of rabbits.

"Under the Spreading Palo Verde, the Desert Biffy Stands." C.T. Art Colortone, *circa 1940s, $7-9.*

Palo Verde Tree in bloom. C.T. Art Colortone, *circa 1940s, $4-6.*

Yucca

Yuccas are also called Desert Candles or Spanish bayonet. While many people call yucca a cactus because they grow in the upper elevations of the Sonoran Desert, it is actually a member of the lily family. Yuccas are pollinated by the yucca moth. Out of the bottom clump of pointed green leaves, a single, rapidly-growing stalk emerges in the spring and produces a beautiful plume of creamy white flowers. The yucca was of major importance to Arizona's Native Peoples who dried and split the leaves for weaving ropes, mats, baskets, sandals, and cloth. The roots of the yucca can be used to make soap.

Yuccas: the Four sisters, the Lord's Candles. C.T. Art Colortone, distributed by Frasher's Inc., *circa 1940s, $4-6.*

Chapter Three:

Animals and Birds

Lunch time in Arizona. In many areas, the burros were turned loose and became wild burros which multiplied in great numbers. They can be destructive to the ecosystem and their constant braying is annoying. C.T. American Art Colored, Harry Herz, Phoenix, Arizona, *circa 1920, $7-9.*

An Arizona Freight Train. Burros were introduced into the Southwest by the Spaniards. The shaggy, hardy little animals proved themselves indispensable as pack animals to cross the desert or to pull heavy loads in mining operations. Benham Indian Trading Company, *circa 1910, $12-14.*

An Arizona Bobcat. Bobcats prowl a territory of one to three miles searching for small mammals and birds. While they rarely attack humans, they are a threat to small pets. Artist R.S. Reed, *1921, $12-15.*

Bobcat. Bobcats are found in all parts of Arizona. They are usually seen alone and are primarily nocturnal. An adult bobcat weighs between fifteen and thirty-five pounds and can jump to heights of twelve feet. *Circa 1940s, $10-12.*

Coyote

While they are called coyotes in the American West, they are sometimes called Prairie Wolves in other areas. They usually travel in packs and hunt in pairs. They have the ability to run at speeds of twenty-five to thirty miles per hour and jump to amazing heights. They will dig and live in dens in the ground or they will utilize a den that another animal has dug. Coyotes tend to be nocturnal and are called scavengers because they will dine on small rodents and plant materials such as mesquite beans. While in some areas a coyote's coloring may be grey, in the Sonoran Desert, coyotes have adapted to a light tan coloring that allows them to blend with their desert surroundings. They weigh about thirty- to forty-pounds and mate for life. Coyotes are legendary in the West for their mournful howls, yips, and yaps at a high pitch. Arizona's Native Peoples tell many folk tales about the coyote, which most often appears as a curious trickster and whose cunning ways ensure its survival.

Coyote, the Desert Outlaw. Coyotes are members of the canine or dog family, and are found throughout North and Central America. C.T. Art Colortone, *circa 1940s, $7-9.*

Jackrabbits

Jackrabbits (hares) avoid the hottest part of the day and feed during the early morning or at dusk. They live on the open ground and are constantly moving, as opposed to cottontail rabbits that live and protect their young underground. Jackrabbit babies are born with their eyes open and with fur. As adults, jackrabbits can reach a length of twenty-five inches. A combination of fast running and leaps helps them when they're being chased by predators. Jackrabbits have good peripheral vision because their eyes are set on the sides of their heads, and their long ears can pick up the sounds of approaching predators. They will drink water if it is available, but they prefer to get moisture from grasses, prickly pear pads, and shrubs.

Aint' We Got Fun! This Cowgirl riding Jackrabbit is an example of exaggeration postcards featuring cowboys or cowgirls riding giant jackrabbits or jackrabbits wearing cow horns or antlers; these types of postcards are still being produced and marketed as Southwestern humor. RPPC by F.D. Conrad, *circa 1940s, $15-18.*

Javelina

Javelina (Collard Peccary) first lived in the tropical climate of southern Argentina and Central America and can be found as far north in Arizona as Yavapai County. The Arizona Department of Game and Fish estimates that there are as many as 60,000 javelinas in Arizona. Javelina can be hunted by obtaining a license and a permit. Javelinas have very poor eyesight. They feed at night and seek shade during the heat. In the Sonoran Desert, javelina feed on prickly pear cacti and hedgehog, but in higher elevations they forage for nuts, flowers, bulbs, berries, and occasionally eggs and carrion. An adult javelina can eat up to three pounds of prickly pear cactus a day. Javelinas have oil glands that emit a strong foul smell, and they mark their territory by rubbing their oily fluid against rocks and trees. If food supply is plentiful, javelinas breed twice a year and most often have litters of two. Babies weigh about one pound and are able to follow their family group in a few days. When the need to defend arises, a javelina will charge head on, biting and locking jaws with a predator.

Javelina Pig—Arizona Wild Life. *While commonly called a pig, the javelina is a Collard Peccary. RPPC, *circa 1951, $8-10.*

Young Javelina near Tucson, Arizona. Adults weigh between thirty-five and sixty pounds and have a mixed coloring of black, gray and brown fur. Tichnor Quality Views, *1944, $5-7.*

Mule Deer

The Mule Deer was named for its long mule-like ears, which have the ability to move independently. While closely related to the White-Tail Deer, Mule Deer are larger and have a black-tipped tail. An adult male (buck) can weigh up to three hundred pounds on hoof, while a female (doe) can weigh up to 175 pounds. Mule Deer prefer warmer, drier habitats and eat primarily grasses in desert regions. They are usually found in small herds and can live up to ten years in the wild.

Mule Deer in Tucson Mountain Park, Arizona. Real Picture Postcard, *circa 1951, $5-7.*

Young Deer in Tucson Mountain Park, Arizona. Tichnor Quality Views, *1944, $5-7.*

George L. Mountainlion Memorial, Arizona-Sonora Desert Museum. Bob Petley, *circa 1959, $4-6.*

Mountain Lion

A 2007 report by the Arizona Game and Fish Department made a reasonable guess that roughly 2,500 to 3,000 Mountain Lions were roaming Arizona. They can be found in many parts of Arizona and have a life span of about thirteen years in the wild. Males weigh between fifty to seventy pounds and range from five to eight feet long. Kittens are usually litters of two. Mountain Lions hunt elk, deer, javelina, and rabbits. They are secretive and shy in nature, therefore few people ever see a Mountain Lion in the wild.

Roadrunners

Roadrunners are the "clowns of the desert," speeding away at eighteen miles per hour, only to stop short. While a roadrunner can fly, it prefers to run along the ground and will race alongside of an automobile. After a strange, frenzied mating dance, a female will build a nest of twigs high off the ground and will usually bear six to seven chicks. A roadrunner is sometimes called a snake killer, however, they most often eat spiders, scorpions, and lizards. A roadrunner won't back down from a rattler and can side step away quickly from the strike of a rattler.

Road Runner and Rattle Snake in a Finish Battle. E.C. Kropp Co., *circa 1930s, $6-8.*

Gila Woodpeckers

Gila Woodpeckers have brown faces, and black and white backs. Adult males have a red cap on their heads. Their strong neck muscles and long pointed beaks allow them to peck upon hard objects. Woodpeckers are annoying to homeowners who awaken to their persistent drumming, but woodpeckers thrive on wood boring insects such as termites. Woodpeckers also eat nuts and berries, and many choose to make their nests by drilling holes in saguaro cacti.

Gila Woodpecker on Saguaro, Dexter Press, *circa 1959, $6-8.*

Gambel's Quail

Both the male and female Gambel's Quail have pear shaped bodies and a plume or topknot on top of their heads. Both males and females have an average weight of six ounces and a wingspan of about fourteen inches. Gambel's Quail are ground feeders and will forage in the early mornings and early evenings for seeds, grasses, berries, and shrubs. There is a link between their reproduction and the amount of rainfall. In years of abundant rainfall, a female will lay more eggs. Though each female lays many eggs, their survival rate is low. Chicks (affectionately called walnuts with wings) follow behind adults, and when adults call out warnings of approaching danger, they will run or fly into low brush for concealment.

Gambel's Quail at Waterhole. *This postcard has the strangest colored quail. Gambel's quail are actually brown, with tan, white and black markings. Color King Natural Color Card, *circa 1959, $6-8.*

Chapter Four:

Creepy Critters

A Desert Tragedy. C.T. Art Colortone, *circa 1940s, $5-7.*

Denizen of the Desert, Gila Monster. The Gila Monster is the largest lizard found in North America and can grow to a length of twenty-two inches. C.T. Art Colortone, *circa 1940s, $4-6.*

Gila Monsters

Gila Monsters are poisonous large lizards. Because of their size and bright coloring, Gila Monsters are easy to see, and they are usually sluggish and slow moving. A Gila monster uses its forked black tongue to scent the air. It moves about on four short legs from which its toes extend. Gila Monsters, rattlesnakes, and Western coral snakes are the only venomous reptiles found in the Sonoran Desert.

Family of Gila Monsters on a Stump. Gila Monsters are bright colored in shades of coral and black. Their scales give them the appearance of being beaded. *Circa 1940s, $4-6.*

Horned Toad or Horned Lizard. Horned Toads have a round flat body, with a crown of thorns on the back of their heads. C.T. American Art Colored, *circa 1930s, Harry Herz, Phoenix, Arizona, $5-7.*

Horned Toads

Horned Toads (Horny Toads or Horned Lizards) have the ability to blend perfectly into areas of rock and sand. They can grow to lengths of six inches and have hair-like projections at the edge of their sides and stubby tails, which prevent a shadow. They have the very strange defense system of being able to squirt blood from the corners of their eyes when threatened. This blood is noxious to coyotes, wolves, and dogs. They can puff themselves up to appear larger if under attack. Horny toads move slowly, and although they eat a variety of other insects, their favorite food is harvester ants. They are smart enough to not eat so many ants as to attract the attention of the colony and provoke an attack or to cause the colony to move. Unfortunately since man is trying to eradicate ants, the Horny Toad population is declining.

Horned Toad and Young.
C.T. Art Colortone, *circa 1940s, $4-5.*

A Desert Rattler Ready to Strike. C.T. American Art Colored, *circa 1930s, $8-10.*

Rattlesnakes

As funny as it sounds, the easiest way to tell if a snake is a rattlesnake is the presence of a rattle. As a rattlesnake matures and sheds its skin, new segments are added to its flesh colored rattle, which a rattler uses to warn off predators. Western Diamondback Rattlers, Black-tail Rattlers, the Mohave Rattlesnake, and the Sidewinder are found in the Sonoran Desert. One myth about rattlesnakes is that they need to be coiled to strike. A rattler's fangs allow it to inject its prey with venom, which has the ability to break down cells and tissue, therefore causing respiratory failure or paralysis. Rodents, squirrels, small rabbits, and birds are a rattler's chosen prey. A rattler has poor eyesight, so they use their tongues to test the air for sensory signals. While there are lots of stories about humans and rattlesnake bites, only a very small portion of those who are bitten by a rattler die, and in most cases, a rattler isn't aggressive. The best way to avoid a rattlesnake bite is to freeze and then slowly back away. Unfortunately, many people believe that taking a closer look or poking a rattler with a stick might be fun—then they suffer a bite. Babies are born alive in liters and will remain in the den with their mother until they shed their first skin in about ten days.

A Lonesome Rattler. Natural Color Postcard, E.C. Kropp Co., *circa 1940, $10-12.*

Section Three: Working the Land

Desert Treasures, Tucson, Arizona,
RPPC, *1949, $7-9.*

Chapter Five:

Citrus & Date Farming

Oranges in Arizona. The unusual feature of this tree is that it bears fruit and blooms at the same time. Bob Petley, *circa 1950, $4-6.*

Citrus Groves

Citrus fruit has been grown in Southern Arizona for over one hundred years, and given the fact that heat produces sugar in citrus, Arizona produces some of the sweetest citrus. Too much sunlight can damage the leaves and trunks of citrus trees, so a citrus tree will grow branches to the ground to protect its trunk from sunburn. Grove managers top the citrus trees now, but the ground branches are left alone. Citrus trees grown for private use are usually trimmed by landscapers, and the tree trunks should be painted white to protect them. Citrus trees can tolerate some cold weather, but great care must be taken to cover citrus if there is a possibility of frost.

Roadside citrus stands were common in Tucson and Yuma where customers could buy several different varieties of oranges, grapefruit, and lemons individually or by the crate. The citrus stands also sold desert and orange blossom honeys and various kinds of dates. A few citrus stands are still in existence. Many of Tucson's citrus groves are gone, and Yuma's citrus has declined somewhat, but Maricopa County has increased its citrus production. Today, South American countries and Australia provide much of the citrus that enters the United States. Arizona ranks fourth in citrus production in the U.S., behind Florida, California, and Texas.

Clusters of Grapefruit. Distributed by R.E.Simpson, *circa 1930, $6-8.*

Citrus in Arizona. Arizona's soil is perfect for growing citrus when it is irrigated. Color King Card, *circa 1955, $4-6.*

An Irrigated Orange Grove, Arizona. C.T. Art Colored, Harry Herz, *circa 1930s, $4-6.*

Date Palms. Furgasons Drug Store, Yuma, Arizona, *1910, $6-8.*

Date Farming

Date palms are possibly the oldest cultivated trees, and dates are one of the most expensive, labor intensive, fruit crops. Spanish friars are credited with bringing the first date palms to the gardens of the missions along the California coastline, but the date palm failed to thrive because there was too much moisture. One oddity about the date palm is that while rain is its enemy, its shallow root system requires a shocking amount of water. Because planting date seeds would produce a new variety each time, propagating the offshoots of a date palm is required to reproduce the same variety. One male date palm and forty-eight female date palms are planted thirty feet apart per acre. Since nature did not make adequate provisions for pollinating female date palms, pollination is accomplished by removing the flowers of the male and sprinkling the pollen on the female date berries by hand. The ripening dates must be thinned and covered, and the palm fronds must be de-thorned to protect the date grove cultivators. As if growing dates isn't complicated enough, the dates ripen on the stalks at different times, so the dates are picked by hand. In the past, ladders were attached to the palms for the workers to climb, but now most growers use booms mounted on trucks. A mature female palm can produce about 150-300 pounds of dates each year. It is estimated that Arizona produces about five percent of the dates grown in the United States.

Twelve Bunches Will Average Fifty Pounds. RPPC, *1913, $10-12.*

How Dates Grow in Arizona. R.L. Balke Indian Trading Co., Phoenix, Arizona, *1909, $7-9.*

Greyhound Bus Stop, Dateland, Arizona. Dateland was established as a railroad water stop in the 1920s and progressed to a favorite stopping place when traveling between Yuma and Phoenix. RPPC, *circa 1949, $10-12.*

Dateland, Arizona. Dateland is still a date grove where travelers can purchase premium dates and date shakes. RPPC, *circa 1925, $8-10.*

Date Palms in Arizona. Arizona's climate, which is similar to Egypt's, is conducive to raising this delicious fruit that is often called Nature's Candy. Bob Petley, *circa 1950, $4-6.*

Chapter Six:

Dude Ranches

The first tenderfoots, greenhorns, or dudes were young men from the east sent to cattle ranches in the Arizona Territory by parents who hoped that the experience would "make a man out of them" or who believed that their sons would have a better life and more opportunities in the West. Volumes have been written about how hard life was for the cowboy, but Western films of the 1930s featuring "film" or "drugstore" cowboys were immensely popular.

Guest or dude ranches first began appearing in the late 1920s, after the decline of large-scale cattle ranching in Arizona. It allowed visitors to experience life on a ranch with horses, cattle, and cowboys. Some dude ranches expected guests to help with the ranch chores, but as history writer Thomas Sheridan wryly stated in *Arizona, A History*, most visitors wouldn't have wanted to stretch barbed wire or castrate calves. Dude ranch vacations usually included relaxing in the sun next to a swimming pool, trail rides that ended with a steak fry, entertainment by singing cowboys, square dances, watching wildlife, talks on the history of the area, and side trips to Indian ruins and ghost towns. Guests often wore very fancy western shirts, Stetson hats, chaps, and other items of clothing similar to that of their favorite Hollywood cowboy or cowgirl. Because of the extreme weather in Southern Arizona, most of the dude ranches operated during the months of October to May. *Arizona, The Grand Canyon State, A State Guide* stated that there were more than three hundred dude ranches operating in Arizona in 1966, but only a handful are still in operation today. Most are called guest ranch resorts, and their list of amenities is impressive. Still, one can't help but wonder what the old cowboys and dude ranch wranglers would have thought of spa services, vegan foods, and wireless Internet on a ranch.

Circle Z Ranch.
RPPC, *circa 1952*,
$10-12.

Panorama of Circle Z Guest Ranch, Patagonia, Arizona. C.T. American Art Colored, Harry Herz, *circa 1930, $7-9.*

Saddlin' Up at a Desert Dude Ranch. C.T. Art Colortone, *circa 1940s, $4-6.*

Typical Arizona Ranch Scene, Loma Vista Ranch.
C.T. Art Colortone, *circa 1940s, $4-6.*

On a Southern Arizona Guest Ranch, Rock Island Railroad.
E.C. Kropp Co., *circa 1940s, $8-10.*

Cielo Tierra Guest Ranch, Tucson, Arizona. Real Picture Postcard, *circa 1950, $10-12.*

The Sahara. Tucson's finest guest ranch on Orange Grove Road. Photocraft, *1955, $10-12.*

Roundup House, Rincon Ranchito, Tucson, Arizona. Real Picture Postcard, *1949, $10-12.*

Front Terrace, Rancho de la Osa. Named for the black bears that once roamed the area, Rancho de la Osa is located along the Mexican border near Sasabe, Arizona. Famous guests include Zane Grey, Tom Mix, President and Mrs. Lyndon Johnson. The sender of this postcard mentions her stay of nine weeks on the ranch, and the excitement of seeing 1,000 cattle coming to the ranch from Mexico. *Circa 1958, $8 -10.*

Triple H Ranch Inn, Tucson, Arizona. RPPC, Dexter Press Silvercraft, *circa 1953, $12-14.*

Fashion Show, Wild Horse Guest Ranch, Tucson, Arizona. Natural Color Card, *circa 1955, $8-10.*

Chapter Seven:

Mining Towns

Long before Arizona was known as the Grand Canyon State, it was called the Copper State. In fact, the five-pointed copper colored star in the center of the Arizona state flag was chosen to represent Arizona's tremendous copper industry.

Very early miners in Arizona had little equipment beyond their picks, shovels, and a strong burro to carry their ore to the assay office. Later, miners would use sticks of dynamite, sledgehammers, picks, drills, and ore cars. Miners hoped to find gold and silver—and some did—but by 1888, copper mining had surpassed gold and silver mining. Arizona would lead the U.S. copper production for most of the twentieth century.

Ajo

Ajo, pronounced "Ah hoe," is located about 130 miles west of Tucson and 120 miles southwest of Phoenix. Ajo, which means garlic in Spanish, grows wild in the hills in the surrounding area; that offers one explanation of how the town was named. Others suggest that the name came from the Papago word "Auauho" (paint) since the Papago (now Tohono O'odham) used the red ore pigment to paint their bodies. The tribal land of the Tohono O'odham is located east of Ajo.

The Spanish mined rich deposits of ore found near Ajo as early as 1750. In 1864, Ajo became the site of the first American-operated mine in Arizona when pioneers Charles Poston and Pete Brady organized the American Mining and Trading Company after large deposits of low grade copper, streaked with deposits of high grade "ruby" copper, was discovered. The copper ore was carried by pack mules to Yuma, shipped down the Colorado River, and around Cape Horn to Swansea, Wales where the copper was smelted. Getting the copper ore smelted was only one problem. Cave-ins, injuries, floods, fires, mine strikes, and price fluctuations plagued the mines, and many promising bodies of ore eventually "played out."

In 1910, John C. Greenway, who had served with Theodore Roosevelt's Cavalry unit, the Rough Riders, during the Spanish American War, came to Bisbee, Arizona to manage the Calumet and Arizona mines. Greenway later became the principal stockholder in the New Cornelia Copper Company near Ajo. When Greenway and his associates engineered a new method of crushing and extracting copper from lower grades of ore, the New Cornelia mine became Arizona's first open pit mining operation. Greenway and his wife, Isabella, designed the town of Ajo. In the heart of Ajo is the Plaza, an open green area surrounded by palm trees and buildings designed in Spanish Colonial Revival architecture. Curley School opened in 1919 for the children of miners, as did a hospital. The Ajo train depot was built in 1915 and served the Tucson, Cornelia, and Gila Bend Railway. While copper prices fell to less than six cents a pound during the Depression in the early 1930s, it rebounded during World War II. As in other Arizona mining towns, the population of Ajo varied with the price of copper. Because Ajo is situated on the road to Rocky Point, Mexico, and is close to the Organ Pipe Cactus National Monument and the Cabeza Prieta National Wildlife Refuge, it is a popular place for travelers to stop.

Business District, on the Plaza, Ajo, Arizona. RPPC, circa 1949, $20-22.

Open Pit Copper Mine, Ajo, Arizona, RPPC, *circa 1950, $12-15.*

High School, Ajo, Arizona. RPPC, *1952, $12-14.*

Hotel Cornelia, Ajo, Arizona. Mrs. John Stone was the manager here. Albertype Co., *circa 1940, $10-12.*

Ajo, Arizona. RPPC, *circa 1949, $15-18.*

Immaculate Conception Catholic Church, Ajo, Arizona. Real Picture Postcard, *circa 1950, $10-12.*

Bisbee

Bisbee was once known as "The Queen of the Copper Camps." U.S. Army scout Jack Dunn discovered copper deposits in the Mule Mountains in 1877, but was swindled out of his claim by Prospector George Warren, and the area around Bisbee became one of Arizona's largest producers of copper. George Warren got his "just desserts" when he lost his partial claim to the Copper Queen Mine by betting that he could outrun a horse during one of his drinking bouts. According to several sources, the amount that his share of the Copper Queen Mine was worth over time was estimated to have been millions. In 1880, Dr. James Douglas came to Arizona as a geologist for the tiny Phelps Dodge & Company. His reports that low-grade copper could be mined at a profit drew him to move to Bisbee in 1889. Along with his partners, Douglas would play a large role in the development of the Copper Queen Mine and the formation of the El Paso and Southwestern Railroad, making James Douglas one of Arizona's leading men in mining. Lead and zinc deposits were also mined. The Calumet & Arizona mine was organized by Captain Jim Houston who had other mining operations in Bisbee and Warren. A third mining company, the Shattuck-Arizona-Copper Company, was formed. Eventually, the Phelps Dodge & Company would buy the other Bisbee area mining interests.

The town of Bisbee was named for Judge DeWitt Bisbee whose son-in-law owned an interest in the Copper Queen Mine, yet the Judge *never* actually visited the town. One of the most famous sections of Bisbee was Brewery Gulch, which began at the Mulheim Brewery and continued up the saloon-lined canyon to the brothels near the top of the canyon. A city ordinance in 1902 banned women from Bisbee's saloons, but other city ordnances allowed for a red light district and the regulation and taxation of prostitution. It was said that the higher up Brewery Gulch one went, the wilder it was.

Portion of the Business Section, Bisbee, Arizona. C.T. Art Colored, Harry Herz, Phoenix, Arizona, *1932, $8-10.*

Naco Road, showing El Paso and Southwestern Depot, Bisbee, Arizona. Naco Road connects the towns in the Warren Mining District and is the main highway to Douglas. C.T. American Art, *circa 1938, $12-15.*

Welfare Factories of the Warren Mining District. Y.M.C.A Men's Building, Boys Department, Bisbee, Arizona. Curt Teich & Co., Chicago, Illinois, *circa 1930s, $10-12.*

Main Street, Bisbee, Arizona. C.T. Art Colortone, *circa 1940s, $6-8.*

Castle Rock, Entrance to Tombstone Canyon, Bisbee, Arizona. C.T. Art Colortone, *circa 1940s, $6-8.*

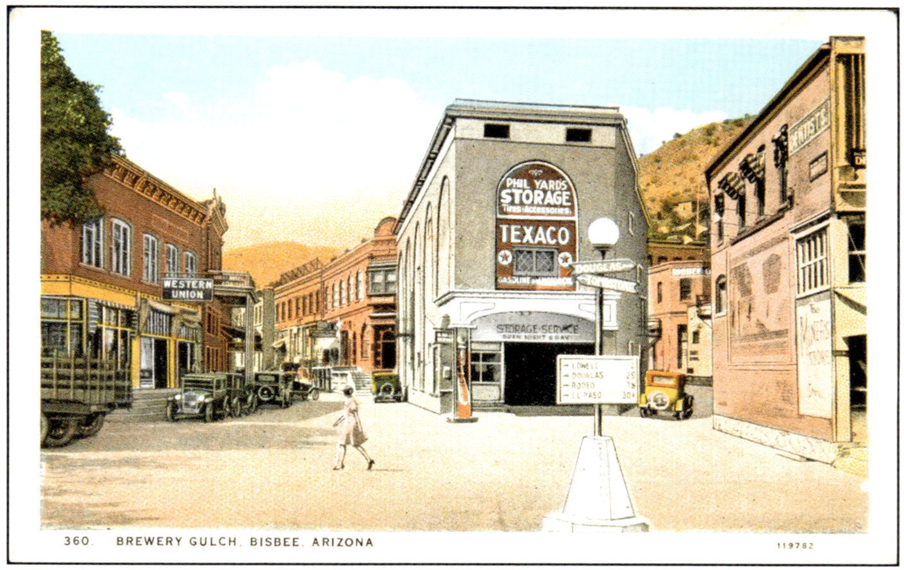

Brewery Gulch, Bisbee, Arizona. This well known place was formerly known as Mule Gulch. C.T. American Art Colored, *circa 1930s, $8-10.*

Castle Rock, Bisbee, Arizona. RPPC, *circa 1950, $9-11.*

Youngblood Hill, Bisbee, Arizona. RPPC, *circa 1950, $9-11.*

Castle Rock and Business District, Bisbee, Arizona. *Circa 1950, $9-11.*

Brewery Gulch, Bisbee Arizona. Once the boisterous stronghold of miners' revelry. John Ball Photo, C.T. Art Colortone, *circa 1940s, $6-8.*

The Historic Old Brewery. Brewery Gulch with Pythian Castle in the background, Bisbee, Arizona. Frasher's Fotos, *circa 1951, $10-12.*

Bisbee was once known as "The Queen of the Copper Camps." U.S. Army scout Jack Dunn discovered copper deposits in the Mule Mountains in 1877, but was swindled out of his claim by Prospector George Warren, and the area around Bisbee became one of Arizona's largest producers of copper. George Warren got his "just desserts" when he lost his partial claim to the Copper Queen Mine by betting that he could outrun a horse during one of his drinking bouts. According to several sources, the amount that his share of the Copper Queen Mine was worth over time was estimated to have been millions. In 1880, Dr. James Douglas came to Arizona as a geologist for the tiny Phelps Dodge & Company. His reports that low-grade copper could be mined at a profit drew him to move to Bisbee in 1889. Along with his partners, Douglas would play a large role in the development of the Copper Queen Mine and the formation of the El Paso and Southwestern Railroad, making James Douglas one of Arizona's leading men in mining. Lead and zinc deposits were also mined. The Calumet & Arizona mine was organized by Captain Jim Houston who had other mining operations in Bisbee and Warren. A third mining company, the Shattuck-Arizona-Copper Company, was formed. Eventually, the Phelps Dodge & Company would buy the other Bisbee area mining interests.

The town of Bisbee was named for Judge DeWitt Bisbee whose son-in-law owned an interest in the Copper Queen Mine, yet the Judge *never* actually visited the town. One of the most famous sections of Bisbee was Brewery Gulch, which began at the Mulheim Brewery and continued up the saloon-lined canyon to the brothels near the top of the canyon. A city ordinance in 1902 banned women from Bisbee's saloons, but other city ordnances allowed for a red light district and the regulation and taxation of prostitution. It was said that the higher up Brewery Gulch one went, the wilder it was.

Sacramento Pit, Bisbee, Arizona. C.T. Art Colortone, *circa 1940s, $6-9.*

Cochise County Courthouse and St. Patrick's Catholic Church, Bisbee, Arizona. The Courthouse was constructed in 1931 by the Clinton Cambell Construction Company. RPPC, *circa 1950s, $10-12.*

Public School, Bisbee, Arizona. *Circa 1908. $7-9.*

Loretto Academy and St. Patrick's Catholic Church, Bisbee, Arizona. *One can only wonder what the writer of this postcard meant when she wrote to her mama, "Of course Bisbee is no good." The Academy is located alongside the church. Benham Company, Los Angeles, *1912, $10-12.*

Copper Queen Hotel, Bisbee, Arizona.
An elegant hotel, built in 1902, by the Copper Queen Consolidated Mining Company at a cost of $75,000. A.O. Bores Co., Phoenix, Arizona, *circa 1920s, $6-8.*

Copper Queen Hospital, Bisbee, Arizona. Benham Company, Los Angeles, *circa 1912, $10-12.*

Copper Queen Hotel and Northern European Gothic Style Presbyterian Church. Real Picture Postcard, *circa 1950, $10-12.*

Country Club, Warren District, Arizona. HHT Company, *circa 1930s, $7-9.*

Douglas

Douglas is located along Arizona's southeastern border in the Sulphur Springs Valley and across the United States border from Agua Prieta, Sonora, Mexico. Dr. James Douglas, who played a large role in the development of the Phelps Dodge Copper Queen Mine in Bisbee, moved the mine's smelting operations to the town of Black Water, which later was renamed Douglas in honor of Dr. Douglas. The Copper Queen Smelter processed ore from mines in Bisbee, Jerome, and Nacozari, Mexico. A second smelter was constructed in Douglas by the Calumet and Arizona Mine, which became a reduction plant when Phelps Dodge bought its mining interests.

Hotel Gadsden, Douglas, Arizona. RPPC, *circa 1940s, $10-12.*

"G" Avenue looking North, Douglas, Arizona. Lithochrome printed in Germany, Douglas Drug Store, *circa 1908, $20-25.*

South toward Mexico on "G" Avenue, Douglas, Arizona. C.T. Art Colortone, *circa 1940s, $6-8.*

Tenth Street from "G" Avenue, Douglas, Arizona. Real Picture Postcard, *circa 1940s, $15-20.*

First National Bank, Douglas, Arizona. Benham Indian Trading Co., Los Angeles, California, *1908, $8-10.*

Presbyterian Church, Douglas, Arizona. Tenth Street Curio Store, made in Germany, *circa 1909, $8-10.*

Episcopal Church, Douglas, Arizona. Tenth Street Curio Store, made in Germany, *circa 1909, $8-10.*

First Baptist Church, Douglas, Arizona. Real Picture Postcard, *circa 1955, $7-9.*

Country Club, Douglas, Arizona. E.C. Kropp Co., *circa 1930s, $8-10.*

County Hospital, Douglas, Arizona. E.C. Kropp Co., *1938, $8-10.*

In 1901, the town of Douglas had the distinction of becoming the home of the newly formed Arizona Rangers to tame lawbreakers who frequented the saloons on both sides of the border. Because of the rich grasslands surrounding Douglas, cattle ranching and cattle shipping made Douglas an important cattle ranching center. Douglas also became known as a prime hunting area for those interested in hunting jaguar. As with many border towns, Douglas did a booming business during Prohibition when tourists came to Douglas and took cabs to Agua Prieta—where the liquor flowed freely. When the smelting operations closed in 1987, Douglas began reinventing itself.

Elks' Home, Douglas, Arizona.
E.C. Kropp Co., *circa 1930s, $8-10.*

Library, Douglas, Arizona.
Newman Postcard Co., Los Angeles, California, made in Germany, *circa 1909, $8-10.*

El Paso and Southwestern Railroad Depot, Douglas, Arizona. The depot was constructed in 1901. S.H. Kress & Co., *circa 1930s, $7-9.*

High School, Douglas, Arizona. HHT Co., *circa 1930s, $8-10.*

School Building, Douglas, Arizona. Douglas Drug Co., made in Germany, *1907, $18-22.*

U.S. Post Office, Douglas, Arizona, RPPC. *Circa 1951, $9-11.*

YMCA, Douglas, Arizona, HHT Co., *circa 1930s, $5-7.*

United States Custom Office, Douglas, Arizona. The small town of Agua Prieta, Sonora, Mexico lies just across the border. RPPC, *circa 1949, $12-15.*

Queen Hotel, Douglas, Arizona. Tenth Street Curio Store, *circa 1907, $9-11.*

Gadsden Hotel, Douglas, Arizona. "The Last of the Grand Hotels," the Gadsden Hotel was named in honor of James Gadsden who engineered the Gadsden Purchase in 1853. The architect was Henry Trost of El Paso, Texas. The Gadsden Hotel was listed on the National Register of Historic Places in 1976. **No date or cost estimate was available.*

View of the Copper Queen Smelter, Douglas, Arizona. Newman Post Card Co., *circa 1910, $4-6.*

Gadsden Hotel, Dining Room, Douglas, Arizona. A gathering place for cattle barons, mining officials, businessmen, and hunters. Humphries Photo Co., El Paso, Texas, *circa 1920, $10-12.*

Gadsden Hotel, Gift Shop, Douglas, Arizona. Humphries Photo Co., El Paso, Texas, *circa 1920, $10-12.*

Lobby, Gadsden Hotel, Douglas, Arizona. The stained glass is by Tiffany and the stairs of Italian marble. F.O. Mackey, owner and operator. Tichnor Quality Views, *circa 1920s, $6-8.*

Cochise Head in Chiricahua Mountains, Arizona.
RPPC, *circa 1955, $6-8.*

Rock Formations, "Wonderland of Rocks," Chiricahua National Monument, Arizona.
C.T. Art Colortone, *circa 1940s, $5-7.*

The Chiricahua National Monument lies to the east of Tombstone and to the north of Douglas in the southeastern corner of Arizona. The relatively moderate climate and the proximity of the Chiricahua National Monument—also known as the "Wonderland of Rocks"—has always attracted a number of tourists to Douglas. The Chiricahua National Monument is an 11,000-acre wonderland of balanced rocks, spires, and hoodoos that were formed when a volcano at Turkey Creek erupted over twenty-seven million years ago and left fused volcanic ash that, over time, eroded into the fantastic formations. The area was home to the Chiricahua Apaches, who were able to effectively use the maze of "standing up" rocks to avoid capture by the U.S. Calvary soldiers. Today hikers, birders, and those interested in the unusual geology frequent the area.

Wonderland of Rocks, Chiricahua National Monument, Douglas, Arizona. The erosive actions of wind and water have carved these rhyolite rock pillars. *Circa 1955, $4-6.*

Wonderland of Rocks, Arizona. RPPC, *1941, $6-8.*

Tombstone

Tombstone is located about seventy miles southeast of Tucson. German prospector, Ed Schieffelin, discovered a rich vein of silver and recorded his claim on September 3, 1877. Because of frequent Apache raids in the area, Schieffelin had been warned that the only thing he would find in the area would be his own tombstone. The name "Tombstone" stuck, and Schieffelin is credited with discovering the richest silver strike in Arizona's history. Schieffelin, though, was a restless man, and he sold his claim in 1880 for $10,000 before stope mining (timber supported underground mining) produced over five million dollars of ore. After a life of adventure, Schieffelin was buried in his prospector's clothing with his pick and shovel—as he had requested—not far from Tombstone, in the area where he had discovered his silver strike.

A post office was established in 1878 in Tombstone, and by 1879, the town site had been developed and lots were being sold for five dollars each in the business district along Allen Street. About fifty mines were operating in the area, and Tombstone grew to a town of 10,000. Tombstone had its share of mining officials, miners, merchants, and regular folks, but gamblers, soiled doves, cowboys, and smugglers also came to Tombstone and trouble flourished. Due to Western films and television shows, most people associate Tombstone with the gunfight at OK Corral that took place on October 26, 1881. Doc Holliday and the Earp brothers stood against the Clantons, the McLowerys, and their outlaw friends called the Cowboys. While many Hollywood stories about the Earps have portrayed them as trying to escape their checkered past by being upstanding lawmen, some historians see the Earps as having conducted questionable dealings in Tombstone while hiding behind their badges.

Allen Street, Tombstone, Arizona. Color Card from Kodachrome, *1958, $5-7.*

Greetings from Tombstone. See Tombstone—"The Town Too Tough To Die." Perfect climate, history, romance… Tombstone, Arizona, has it all. C.T. Colortone, *1931, $7-9.*

Wells Fargo Express Office, Tombstone, Arizona. The original adobe Wells Fargo Express office was built in 1880. Wells Fargo transported gold bullion and silver from the mines. RPPC, *circa 1952, $7-9.*

Schieffelin Monument, Tombstone, Arizona.
RPPC, *circa 1953, $7-9.*

Looking West on Main (Allen) Street, Tombstone, Arizona.
RPPC, *circa 1940s, $7-9.*

Scene on Allen Street, Tombstone, Arizona.
RPPC, *circa 1950, $7-9.*

Bird Cage Theatre

The Bird Cage Theatre opened on Christmas day 1881 and operated around the clock as a vaudeville theater, dance hall, saloon, gambling casino, and brothel. Because of the twelve tiny prostitution "cribs" suspended on the upper level, where the painted ladies entertained gentlemen for $25 behind red velvet curtains, the Bird Cage is thought to have been the inspiration for the Arthur Lamb song, "She was Only a Bird in a Gilded Cage." Two other rooms that were used by the prostitutes were located in the basement. The Bird Cage quickly gained a reputation as the wildest, most wicked establishment between San Francisco and New Orleans. Bartenders poured only the best liquors and fine wines. Faro and roulette were played on the main floor, but a room below the stage in the basement was reserved for a high stakes poker game with a $1,000-buy in. The game was rumored to have never stopped during the eight years that the Bird Cage was open. The poker players included many of the famous, and it's estimated that over ten million dollars changed hands at the poker table with a ten percent fee for the house. This is a fantastic amount, in direct contrast to the fact that most of the miners only earned about four dollars per day for a ten-hour shift. The Bird Cage closed in 1889, but during its short time as a theatre, it was the scene of numerous gun and knife fights that resulted in twenty-six deaths; 149 bullet holes can be found in the ceiling and walls.

When the Bird Cage closed, the doors were locked with the contents intact. The Bird Cage remained undisturbed until it was reopened as a museum in 1934. For anyone interested in the history of the West, the museum walls are lined with photos and paintings of the patrons and performers who spent time at the Bird Cage. The faro table that Doc Holliday set his faro "bank" on is displayed, but the pool table that Morgan Earp was killed on is in storage now because unscrupulous souvenir hunters continued to chip pieces off of it. The hearse, the Black Mariah, that carried the unlucky to Boot Hill, is another popular exhibit at the Bird Cage Museum. The original stage where Josephine Sarah "Sadie Jo" Marcus, the singer, dancer, and probable prostitute, performed is still there with its original painted backdrop. Josephine is said to have become the third Mrs. Wyatt Earp. Other performers at the Bird Cage Theatre included Lotta Crabtree, Lilly Langtree, Lillian Russell, Eddy Foy, and the nightly Cancan dancers. Because of the number of violent deaths that took place at the Bird Cage, rumors of hauntings and other unexplained strange happenings persist, which makes the Bird Cage a popular place for those with an interest in tracking the paranormal. The Bird Cage Theatre is a Registered National Monument.

Bird Cage Theatre, Tombstone, Arizona. This theatre was built in 1881 at a cost of $600 and opened on Christmas Day, 1881. RPPC, *circa 1952, $8-10.*

Bar, Bird Cage Theatre, Tombstone, Arizona. This painting of Fatima, an exotic dancer known as Little Egypt, was placed behind the bar in the Bird Cage Theatre. While Fatima appears to have two belly buttons in the painting, one is actually a bullet hole. RPPC, *circa 1952, $15-20.*

The Black Mariah Hearse, Tombstone, Arizona. Built at a cost of $8,000, the hearse carried bodies to Boot Hill Cemetery. One of only eight in existence, the hearse is inlaid with 14K gold around the windows and has sterling silver trim. The hearse is housed in the Bird Cage Theatre Museum. RPPC, *1944, $7-9.*

Lobby and Bar, Bird Cage Theatre, Tombstone, Arizona. Today, the theatre is the Bird Cage Museum. Real Picture Postcard, *1956, $20-25.*

The Crystal Palace

Crystal Palace Saloon, Tombstone, Arizona.
RPPC, *circa 1940s, $20-25.*

The Famous Crystal Palace Saloon, Tombstone, Arizona.
RPPC, Frashers Foto, *circa 1950, $10-12.*

The original bar of the Crystal Palace Saloon, Tombstone, Arizona.
RPPC, *circa 1940s, $20-25.*

Crystal Palace Bar, Tombstone Arizona.
A scene from Helldorado Days, which is a celebration of Tombstone's past, and hosted by the Tombstone Restoration Commission. Artvue, *1956, $8-10.*

Boot Hill Cemetery

Boot Hill Cemetery humor, Tombstone, Arizona. Here Lies Lester Moore, 4 Slugs from a .44. No Less, No More. RPPC, *circa 1950, $6-8.*

Boot Hill Cemetery, Tombstone, Arizona. This notorious cemetery is where unlucky gunfighters and other townspeople were buried with their boots on. Boot Hill contains about 250 graves. The last burial took place in 1946 and was for Emmett Nunnelley. He was buried there because of his efforts to preserve Book Hill. RPPC, Frashers Foto, *circa 1953, $9-11.*

Boot Hill Cemetery, Tombstone, Arizona. Grave of John Heath, who was the saloonkeeper who led a Tombstone posse down the wrong trail as his part in the Bisbee Massacre. While not sentenced to hang, he was taken from jail and hanged from a telephone pole by an angry Bisbee mob. RPPC, *circa 1950, $6-8.*

City Hall, Tombstone, Arizona. The City Hall was built in a French Renaissance design in 1882. RPPC, *1956, $8-10.*

Visiting Tombstone

Tourists have visited Tombstone for over a century to watch re-enactments of the Earp gunfight and to see the Bird Cage Theatre and the old saloons, such as the Oriental Bar and the Crystal Palace. Like many other western mining towns with mostly wood frame construction, Tombstone suffered devastating fires in 1891 and 1892. Eventually, the underground mines filled with water and the price of silver had fallen to less than $1 per pound, and Tombstone's mining boom was over. Tombstone was only one of many Western towns with a wild and bloody history, but it's certainly one of the best known, having earned the name, "The Town Too Tough to Die." The city of Tombstone was declared a National Historic Landmark in 1962.

The World's Largest Rose Tree, (bush) located at the corner of 4th and Toughnut streets, is a white Lady Banksia rambler variety, which blooms every year in late March or early April just as it always has since it was planted there in 1885. The original root cutting was sent to Mary Gee, who came to Tombstone from Scotland with her husband, Henry, a mining engineer. Mary's family in Scotland sent a box of root cuttings and seeds to the homesick young bride. Some say Mary planted the root and, while other accounts differ, to everyone's surprise, the rose flourished and soon grew large enough that it needed to be supported by wooden posts. By the 1930s, Robert Ripley certified the rose bush as the world's largest in "Ripley's Believe It or Not" and the rose bush now occupies over 8,000 square feet and is listed in the *Guiness Book of World Records.*

Courthouse, Tombstone, Arizona. The two-story brick courthouse, formerly the County Seat of Cochise County, was built in 1882 at a cost of $50,000. The courthouse was turned over to Arizona State Parks in 1959 and is now a museum. RPPC, Frashers Foto, *circa 1950s, $7-9.*

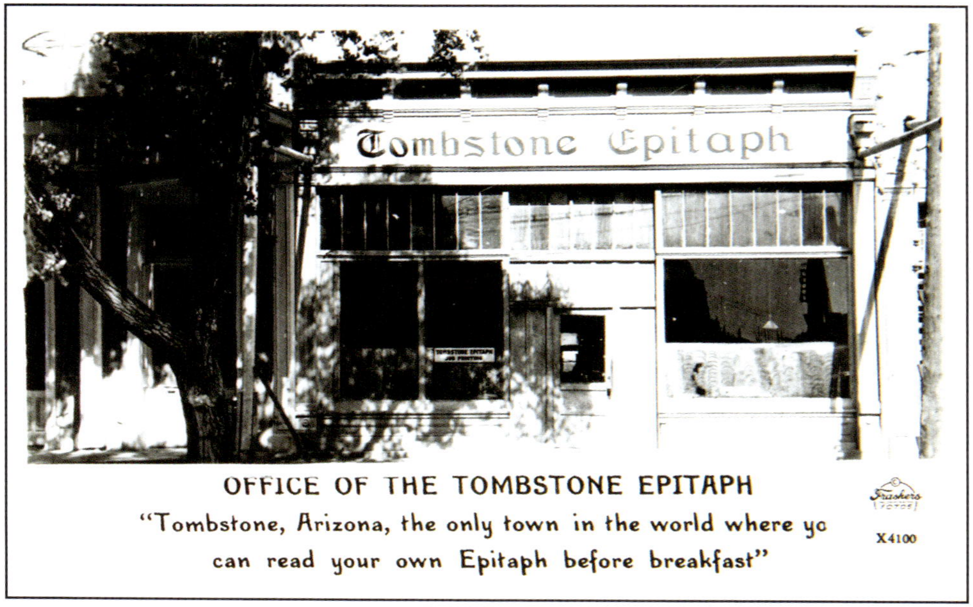

Office of the Tombstone Epitaph. "Tombstone, Arizona, the only town in the world where you can read your own Epitaph before breakfast." John P. Clum, a crusader for law and order in Tombstone, published the first issue of the *Tombstone Epitaph* newspaper on May 1, 1880. Frashers Foto, *circa 1950s, $10-12.*

St. Paul's Episcopal Church, Tombstone, Arizona. St. Paul's was constructed in 1882. RPPC, *circa 1950s, $7-9.*

***Tombstone Epitaph Newspaper*.** Union Oil Company, Natural Color Series of the West, *1950, $6-8.*

World's Largest Rose Bush. This Rose Bush was planted in 1885 in Tombstone, Arizona, and, much to the surprise of everyone, grew and grew and grew. E.C. Kropp Co., *circa 1930s, $4-6.*

Section Four: Out and About

Street Scene in Old Tucson, Tucson, Arizona. This scene is from the Wesley Ruggles film "Arizona" starring Jean Arthur. C.T. Art Colortone, *$6-8*.

Chapter Eight:

Nogales

Nogales (walnuts in Spanish) was named for a grove of black walnut trees in the area that had formerly been part of a Spanish land grant in the fertile Santa Cruz Valley. Nogales is located along the Mexican border about sixty miles south of Tucson and has a "twin city" — Nogales, Sonora, Mexico — directly across the U.S. border. San Francisco merchant Jacob Issacson established a trading post and stage stop in 1880, to serve passengers on the stage line that went from Tucson to Guaymas, Mexico. A community began growing along the boundary line; it was first named "Issacson" and then "Line City." By 1882, the Southern Pacific Railroad passed through the town, which was renamed Nogales. The town became a port of entry and trade center filled with its share of saloons. Life wasn't dull in Nogales. There was trouble with both the Yaqui Indians and bands of guerrilla fighters, such as Pancho Villa and his army from Mexico. After a showdown between Pancho Villa's men and the American National Guardsmen, Villa's men retreated into Mexico. Soon Nogales became one of America's largest centers of exporting produce such as tomatoes, lettuce, and peppers. It is also a center for exporting other merchandise, such as Mexican silver, pottery, furniture, glassware, and leather goods. Ranching, dude ranches, and mining in the area also contribute to the economy of Nogales.

"Twin" Cities. Morley Avenue, Nogales, Arizona, Looking toward Nogales, Mexico. RPPC, *1949, $20-25.*

Morley Avenue, Nogales, Arizona.
The International Drug Co., *1910, $9-11.*

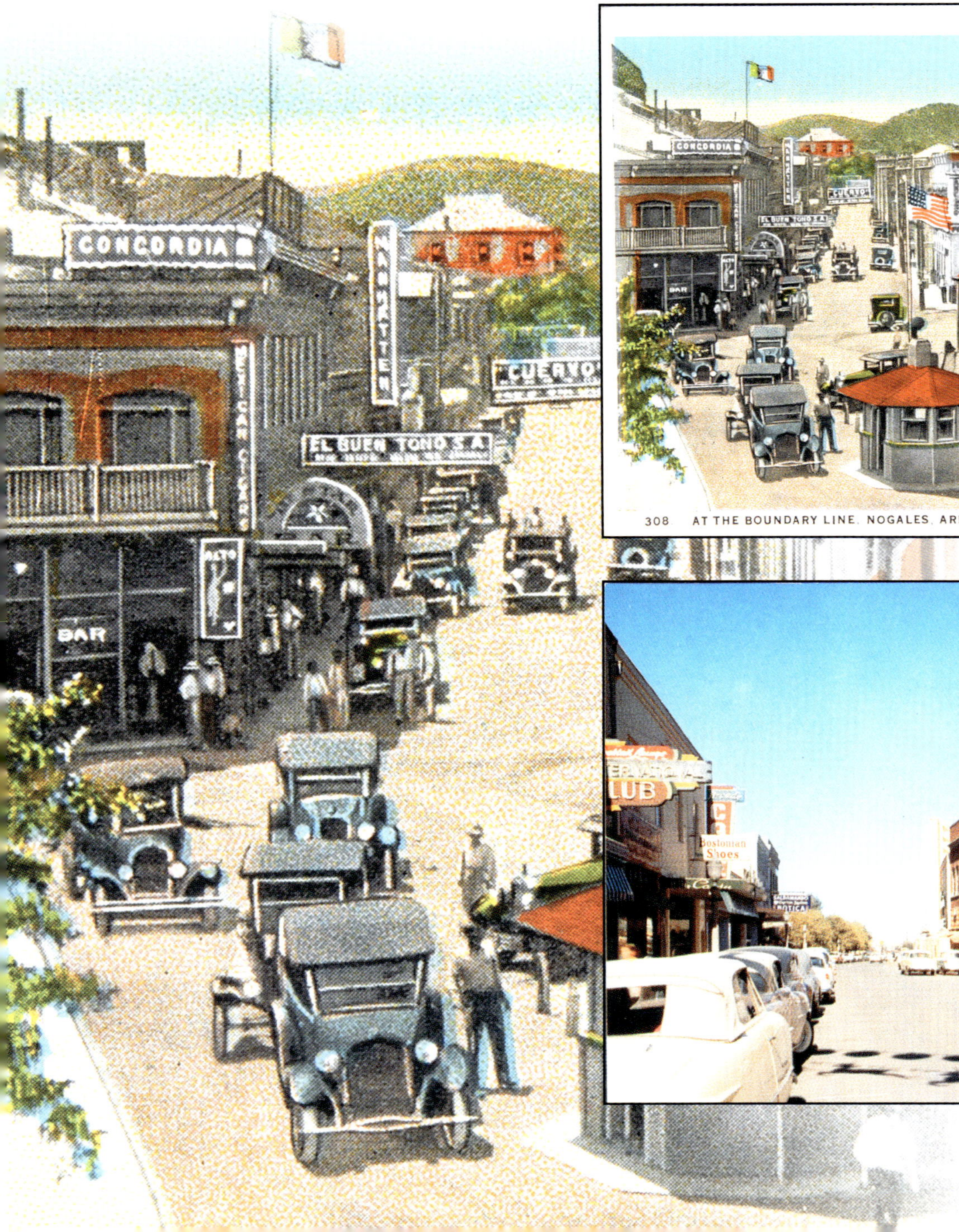

At the Boundary Line, Nogales, Arizona. "Across the Street is Mexico." C.T. American Art Colored, *circa 1930s, $5-7.*

Morley Avenue, Nogales, Arizona. This road is the crossroad of travel between Arizona and Mexico. Petley Studios, *1956, $9-12.*

Santa Cruz County Courthouse, Nogales Arizona. The two-story courthouse was designed by James Vandevort and built at a cost of $28,000 with an additional $4,761 charge for a four-cell jail. The figure on top is Astraea, the Goddess of Justice. RPPC, *circa 1948, $12-15.*

Federal Building, Nogales, Arizona. RPPC, Frashers Fotos, *1936, $15-20.*

Mexican Custom House, Nogales, Arizona. Sonora News Co., *circa 1910, $12-15.*

International Gas Company Works, Nogales, Arizona.
Lithochrome International Drug Co., *1917, $10-12.*

Arizona and Sonora Manufacturing Co., Nogales, Arizona.
Lithochrome International Drug Co., *1916, $10-12.*

The Plaza, Nogales, Arizona. C.T. American Art Colored, *circa 1930s, $5-7.*

Hotel Esplendor, Nogales, Arizona. The Esplendor, which became the Rancho Grande Hotel and Guest Ranch, was built in 1929. The ranch was the film headquarters during the filming of "Red River" and "Oklahoma." C.T. American Art Colored, *circa 1930s, $5-7.*

Residence of Hon. L.W. Mix, Nogales, Arizona. Lithochrome, *1916, $12-15.*

Public school building, Nogales, Arizona. PCK Series, International Drug Co., *1909, $12-15.*

Southern Pacific Depot, Nogales, Arizona. Commerrcial chrome, International Drug Co., *1912, $12-15.*

Titcomb Residence, Nogales, Arizona.
Circa 1930s, $8-10.

Montezuma Hotel, Nogales, Arizona.
Lithochrome International Drug Co., *1916, $8-10.*

Chapter Eight:

Tucson

Nicknamed "the Old Pueblo," Tucson is located in the Santa Cruz Valley, which extends southward to the Mexican border. The Hohokam Native Peoples, who occupied the general area about 2,000 years ago, inhabited the area. The proximity of the Santa Cruz River provided a source of water. As early as 1539, the Spanish moved into the area. (To place Tucson's development into a historical context, Tucson was a developing community before the Pilgrims landed at Plymouth Rock.) Territorial Tucson became a trading and supply center for forts and ranches, and Anglo Americans intermarried with Mexican families. After the Gadsden Purchase, the U.S. Dragoon soldiers were sent to protect the settlement of Tucson, which began attracting more settlers to the area. During the Civil War, Jefferson Davis proclaimed that Arizona was a territory of the Confederacy, and a Confederate cavalry volunteer unit from Texas occupied Tucson. After a brief fight, a Union cavalry unit from California won and the Union proclaimed that Arizona was a U.S. Territory. In 1867, the Arizona Territorial Legislature moved the capitol to Tucson, where it remained for ten years before the it was moved to Prescott.

Congress Street, Tucson, Arizona. The main business thoroughfare of Tucson, the prominent building on right was Valley National Bank. *Circa 1950, $5-7.*

The arrival of the Southern Pacific Railroad in 1880 changed the character of Tucson forever. Suddenly all types of goods became available in less time and, in some cases, at less cost. Lumber, glass, and other building materials replaced adobe construction. Travel by rail was safer, and although it was far from comfortable, it was certainly more comfortable than traveling by horse or wagon. Tucson's sunshine and dry climate made it a perfect place for those suffering from respiratory infections, asthma, rheumatism, and arthritis to receive rest and treatment. The health seekers, who came to Arizona for treatment for tuberculosis, were called consumptives or lungers, and because of the contagious nature of the disease, many of the tourist lodging facilities made it plain in their advertising that they did not take consumptives. In the early days, patients slept in tent sanitariums. Later, desirable sanitariums were designed with sun porches that not only allowed the patients fresh air and sun treatments, but it also provided a ventilation system, which helped to prevent the spread of the disease.

Greetings from Tucson.
C.T. Art Colortone, *circa 1940s, $5-7.*

Bird's Eye View of Tucson, Arizona. C.T. American Art Colored, *1927, $8-10.*

Tucson, Arizona. *Circa 1915, $8-10.*

Congress Street, Tucson, Arizona. C.T. Art Colortone, *1939, $5-7.*

East Congress Street, Tucson, Arizona. E.C. Kropp, *circa 1938, $10-12.*

San Augustin Cathedral and Bishop's Residence, Tucson, Arizona. C.T. Art Colortone, *1955, $6-8.*

A Street in Old Town, Tucson, Arizona. Rasmussen, *circa 1910, $12-15.*

Armory, Tucson, Arizona. E.C. Kropp, *circa 1930s, $6-8.*

First Baptist Church, Tucson, Arizona. RPPC, *1952, $7-9.*

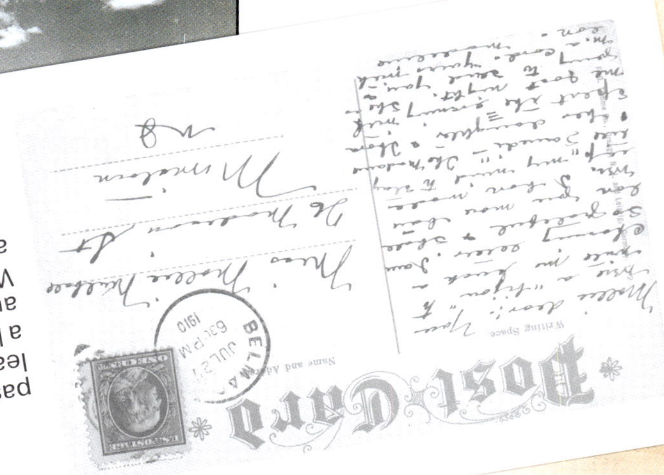

Congregational Church, Tucson, Arizona. The Congregational church organized in 1881 with eight members. S.H. Kress & Co., *circa 1925, $5-7.*

St. Phillip's in the Hills Episcopal Church, Tucson, Arizona. C.T. Art Colortone, *1955, $4-6.*

Latter Day Saints (Mormon) Institute of Religion, Tucson, Arizona. C.T. Art Colortone, *circa 1940s, $5-7.*

Rear View, Pima County Courthouse, Tucson, Arizona. Tichnor Quality Views, *circa 1940, $7-9.*

El Tiradito Shrine, Tucson, Arizona. The El Tiradito, also called the Little Castaway, is a shrine to a sinner rather than a saint, and is commonly called the Wishing Shrine, near downtown Tucson Arizona. One version of the legend of the shrine is that Juan Oliveras fell in love with a married woman who was caught and killed by her husband. It is said that if a candle is lit at night and stays burning until morning, then a wish will be granted.
The sender of this card wrote on the back, "It is a pagan origin to go and put money in a wishing well and your wish will come true." Since candles are always there and there isn't any wishing well, one wonders where the writer of the postcard heard that one! RPPC, *circa 1953, $7-9.*

Pima County Court House, Tucson, Arizona. This was the third Pima County Courthouse. It was designed by Roy W. Place and constructed in a Spanish Colonial style in 1928. The courthouse is still in use. C.T. Art Colortone, *circa 1945, $4-6.*

Scottish Rite Masonic Temple, Tucson, Arizona. E.C. Kropp Co., *circa 1920s, $6-8.*

Owls Men's Club, Tucson, Arizona. This was the second building for the Owls Men's Club. The architect was Henry Trost; it was located at 378 North Main Street. S. H. Kress & Co., *1912, $6-8.*

Carnegie Public Library, Tucson, Arizona. Completed in 1901, it cost of $25,000, which was donated by industrialist Andrew Carnegie. The architect was Henry Trost of El Paso, Texas. *Circa 1902, $6-8.*

City Park Scene, Tucson, Arizona. Albertype Co., *circa 1910, $7-9.*

St. Joseph's Orphanage, Tucson, Arizona. *Circa 1914, $6-8.*

Tucson Senior High School, Tucson, Arizona. Tichnor Bros. Inc., *circa 1930s, $6-8.*

Fort Lowell Adobe Ruins Near Tucson, Arizona. Sandoval News Co./Tucson News Co., *circa 1940s, $5-7.*

The Holiday Public School, Tucson, Arizona. S.H. Kress & Co., *1912, $8-10.*

Marist College, Tucson, Arizona. E.C. Kropp Co., *circa 1920s, $5-7.*

U.S. Post Office, Tucson, Arizona. Frashers Fotos, *circa 1949, $8-10.*

St. Mary's Hospital, established in 1880, Tucson, Arizona.
S.H. Kress & Co., *circa 1912, $14-16.*

St. Mary's Hospital, Sanatorium, and School of Nursing, Tucson, Arizona.
C.T. Art Colortone, *circa 1953, $6-8.*

St. Mary's Hospital and Sanatorium, Tucson, Arizona.
The hospital and sanatorium, today, is under the operation of the Sisters of St Joseph of Carondelet. C.T. Art Colortone, *circa 1943, $6-8.*

"A" Mountain, Southern Pacific Hospital, Tucson, Arizona. "A" Mountain was once the place where sentries kept watch over the tiny pueblo of Tucson. C.T. Art Colortone, *circa 1940s, $4-6.*

U.S. Veteran's Hospital, Tucson, Arizona. The hospital was established for the treatment of tubercular disorders. C.T. Art Colortone, *1937, $8-10.*

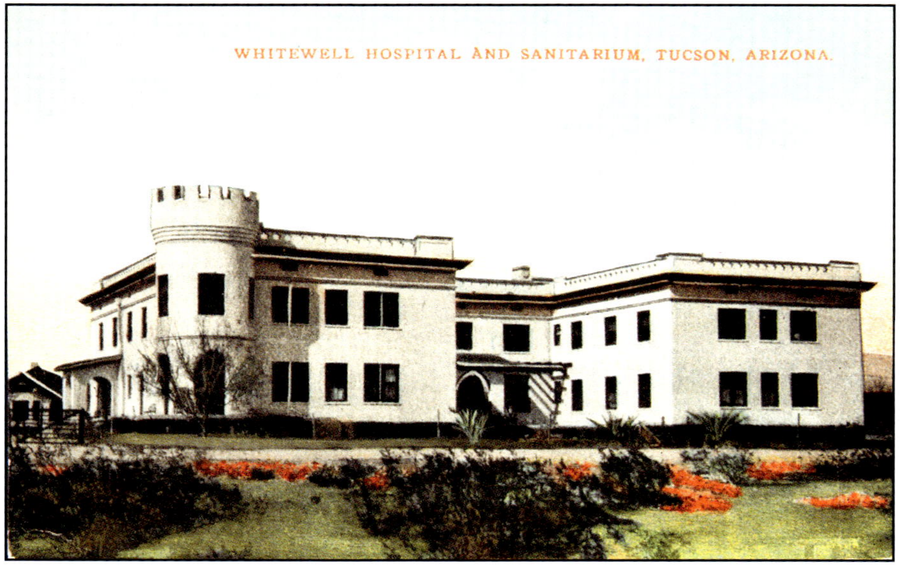

Whitewell Hospital and Sanitarium, Tucson, Arizona.
Circa 1912, $12-15.

City Sights

The Sunshine Climate Club was formed to promote Tucson's tourism. Auto courts that reflected America's auto culture during the 1920s through the 1940s have gone the way of cheap gasoline, but many courts have been restored and a whole "cult" adventure of staying in an auto court has a certain "cool" to today's roadside aficionados. Many had elaborate neon signs in front, shuffleboard courts, play areas, and swimming pools. The auto courts were little gatherings of cottages, each with its own kitchenette and parking space. Many advertised that they were air-cooled, which usually meant a swamp box system of running water through filters and then forcing the cooled air out again. Motels (an abbreviation of motor hotels) came into vogue after auto or tourist courts, and the trend from staying several months in one place was changing to staying a night or two and then traveling on.

Tucson's rodeo, the Fiesta del los Vaqueros, and the rodeo parade were held every February, which was planned to coincide with the height of the tourist season. The Fiesta del los Vaqueros parade was billed as the longest non-mechanized parade in the world. Horse-drawn wagons and carriages, and sheriff's posses on horseback, famous film stars, and marching bands paraded through downtown Tucson. Businesses and schools closed, and Tucson's citizens lined the streets and rooftops to view the rodeo parade. Anyone not wearing western garb ran the risk of being "arrested" by the Chamber of Tucson's vigilantes. The rodeo itself was a far cry from the polished sport that it has become today, and many of the riders were local.

Davis Monthan Air Force Base, located on the southeast side of Tucson, became an important military training center during World War II. Hotels that were formerly brimming with tourists were used as military officers' quarters. The mines in the area surrounding Tucson contributed greatly to Tucson's economy. By 1960, Tucson's population had grown to 265,000. The desire for a "modern" Tucson fueled the destruction of many of Tucson's old adobe buildings and landmarks.

The Donau House, Tucson, Arizona. Built in 1908 at 5 Paseo Redondo, it was demolished in 1965. The architect was Henry Trost. Albertype Co., *1910, $10-12.*

Manning House, Tucson, Arizona. Levi Howell Manning built this modern home, known as the Manning House, in 1907 at 450 West Paseo Redondo, near the heart of downtown Tucson, in an area that was once known as "Snob Hollow." *Circa 1910, $8-10.*

Owls Men's Club, Tucson, Arizona. Construction on the first Owls Club building began in 1899 at 300 North Main Street. Architect Henry Trost designed the Mission Revival Style building. *Circa 1905, $12-15.*

Home on Calle Encanto, Tucson, Arizona. C.T. Art Colortone, *circa 1940s, $4-6.*

Residents strolling Main Street, Tucson, Arizona. C.T. American Art Colored, *1927, $6-8.*

Typical Desert Home, Spanish Type, Tucson, Arizona. Tichnor Brothers Inc., *circa 1930s, $7-9.*

Arizona Inn, Tucson, Arizona. The Inn was built in Spanish style construction in Isabella Greenway's signature colors of pink and blue. With European amenities, the Inn was the first choice for many famous people when in Tucson. C.T. Art Colortone, *circa 1940s, $4-6.*

Arizona Inn, Tucson, Arizona. Isabella Greenway built the Inn in 1930. Sandoval News Co., *circa 1933, $4-6.*

Home of Harold Bell Wright, in Harold Bell Wright Estates, Tucson, Arizona. C.T. American Art, *circa 1930s, $6-8.*

Pioneer Hotel, Tucson, Arizona. Built in 1929 and nicknamed "The Aristocrat of the Desert," the twelve-story hotel was the scene of Arizona's worst fire disaster in 1970. C.T. Art Colortone, *1940s, $6-8.*

El Con Conquistador Hotel, Tucson, Arizona. Completed in 1928, the hotel is situated on 120 acres, with cactus gardens, pool, and riding stables. Sandoval News Co., *circa 1930s, $4-6.*

Patio, Lodge on the Desert, Tucson, Arizona. First built as a residence, the property was converted to a Lodge in 1931. C.T. Art Colortone, *circa 1940s, $5-7.*

Pueblo Hotel and Apartments, formerly the Willard Hotel, Tucson, Arizona. C.T. Art Colortone, *circa 1940s, $8-10.*

Patio of El Presidio Hotel, 4th Avenue and Broadway, Tucson, Arizona. C.T. Art Colortone, *1943, $4-6.*

Santa Rita Hotel, Tucson, Arizona. Built in 1904, the Santa Rita had two hundred rooms and an elevator, which made it a very modern hotel in Territorial Arizona. Jack Parsons Publishing, *circa 1912, $12-15.*

Patio, Geronimo Hotel and Lodge, Tucson, Arizona. Albertype, handcolored, *circa 1915, $12-15.*

Santa Rita Hotel, Tucson, Arizona. Built in 1904, the Santa Rita had two hundred rooms and an elevator, which made it a very modern hotel in Territorial Arizona. Jack Parsons Publishing, *circa 1912, $12-15.*

Arizona Court, 1749 South 6th Avenue, Tucson, Arizona. C.T. Art Colortone, *circa 1940s, $5-7.*

Eagle Courts and Conoco Gas Station, Highway 80, Tucson, Arizona. MWM, color litho, *circa 1930s, $5-7.*

Owl Lodge, 2015 Benson Highway, Tucson, Arizona. Teknitone Process, *circa 1940s, $6-8.*

Sage and Sand Tourist Hotel, 314 Benson Highway, Tucson, Arizona. Teknitone Process, *circa 1940s, $4-6.*

Ghost Ranch Lodge, Tucson, Arizona. Ghost Ranch Lodge was designed by Josias Joesler in 1941. The Catalina Mountains are in the background. Teknitone Process, *circa 1945, $6-8.*

Spanish Trail Motel, U.S. Highway 80, Tucson, Arizona. C.T. Art Colortone, *circa 1940s, $6-8.*

Pool, Tucson Inn, 127 West Drachman Street, Arizona. Natural Color Card, *circa 1958, $5-7.*

Club La Jolla, 1000 South 6th Avenue, Tucson, Arizona. E.C. Kropp, *circa 1930s, $6-8.*

Southern Pacific Railroad Depot, Tucson, Arizona. Completed in 1907, the Depot was recently restored. Harry Hertz, *circa 1930s, $7-9.*

Spanish Type Y.W.C.A. Building, Tucson, Arizona. Tichnor Bros. Inc., *circa 1930s, $6-8.*

Beautiful Spanish Type Southern Pacific Depot, tracks side, Tucson, Arizona. Tichnor Bros. Inc., *circa 1930s, $4-6.*

The Central Dry-In, Stone Avenue and Speedway, Tucson, Arizona.
Natural Color Card, *circa 1958, $10-12.*

Mr. G's Diner & Coffee Shop, 3329 Benson Highway, Tucson, Arizona.
Natural Color Card, *circa 1958, $8-10.*

Sabino Canyon, Tucson, Arizona. The canyon, located near Tucson, is a favorite hiking area. C.T. Art Colortone, *circa 1940s, $4-6.*

Mt. Lemmon

While Mount Lemmon Road begins on the desert floor, the road winds up the mountain to a ski lift reported to be the southernmost ski area in the United States. The small town of Summerhaven is located at the top. Mt. Lemmon is a popular recreational area year around.

Mt. Lemmon Lodge Near Tucson, Arizona. This lodge provides a cool retreat from the summer's heat. RPPC, *circa 1954, $10-12.*

Mt. Lemmon (Hitchcock) Highway, near Tucson, Arizona. C.T. Art Colortone, *circa 1940s, $4-6.*

Mt. Lemmon Highway, Tucson, Arizona. Taking this highway, tourists can go from swimming to skiing in sixty minutes, or Saguaros to Pines, also in sixty minutes. RPPC, *circa 1954, $7-9.*

Old Tucson

Old Tucson was a western film set built in 1939 for the film "Arizona." The set is located west of Tucson in an area that was once reasonably remote. At one time, it was possible to enter Old Tucson and watch film greats such as "Rio Lobo, Rio Bravo," "Gunfight at the OK Corral," "El Dorado," and "Tombstone" being filmed. Many television shows were filmed there too, such as portions of "High Chaparral" and "Little House on the Prairie." Later, amusement rides, shopping, and period performances were added and some terrific western memorabilia was displayed throughout. Sadly, a fire destroyed many of the original wooden film sets and buildings. Old Tucson was reopened and renamed Old Tucson Film Studios, where cowboys perform mock gunfights and rodeos are held. There are also a number of rides and souvenir stores. Occasionally commercials and a few film scenes are filmed there, but the surrounding area has become too populated to make entire feature films.

Interior, Ward's Saloon, Old Tucson, Tucson Mountain Park. Real Picture Postcard, *circa 1950s, $12-15.*

Old Tucson, Arizona. Real Picture Postcard, *circa 1955, $7-9.*

Street Scene in Old Tucson, Tucson, Arizona. This scene is from the Wesley Ruggles film "Arizona" starring Jean Arthur. C.T. Art Colortone, *$6-8*.

Old Tucson, Arizona. This accurate replica of Tucson was built in 1860 for the movie "Arizona." Frashers Fotos, RPPC, *circa 1956, $7-9.*

San Xavier Mission

Padre Eusebio Francisco Kino came to the Santa Cruz Valley to establish several missions in 1687. Kino established a church at Bac, but the original mission was destroyed. After the King of Spain expelled the Jesuit priests from the Spanish Empire, he sent Franciscan priests back to Bac and Franciscan missionary Juan Bautista Velderrain built San Xavier del Bac Mission between 1783 and 1797. The Mission was nicknamed "The White Dove of the Desert" for the white reflective plaster that covered the church's exterior. There are many explanations of why one tower was left unfinished. Wood was scarce in the area, so there was little wood used in the construction except for touches and the massive front doors of mesquite wood. Festivals held at San Xavier have always been a blend of traditional Catholic rites, Hispanic traditions, and Native American ritual dances.

San Xavier Mission, Tucson, Arizona. This view is from a Papago (now Tohono O'odham) Settlement. C.T. Art Colortone, *circa 1940s, $4-6.*

Papago (now Tohono O'odham) School near San Xavier Mission, Tucson, Arizona. *Circa 1915, $12-15.*

San Xavier del Bac Mission, completed circa 1797, near Tucson, Arizona, Albertype. *Circa 1911, $8-10.*

Side Altar, San Xavier Mission, Tucson, Arizona. Creative artists made plaster appear like wood. R. Rasmessen #1, Albertype, handcolored, *circa 1910, $8-10.*

University of Arizona

The University of Arizona was Arizona's first university. The Thirteenth Territorial Legislature established the university, agreeing to provide $25,000 to fund it if the citizens of Tucson would provide forty acres of land. The University of Arizona opened in October of 1891 with six faculty and thirty-six students.

Campus, University of Arizona, Tucson, Arizona. The University — Arizona's first — opened in 1891. C.T. American Art, *circa 1930s, $7-9.*

Agricultural Building, University of Arizona, built in 1915. C.T. American Art, *1934, $6-8.*

Science Building, University of Arizona. E.C. Kropp Co., *circa 1930s, $4-6.*

Memorial Fountain in front of Old Main Building, University of Arizona. C.T. Art Colortone, *1940, $6-8.*

Library and Park, University of Arizona, 1905. Phostint, Detroit Publishing, *1909, $7-9.*

Pima Hall, University of Arizona. This women's dormitory was completed in 1941. C.T. Art Colortone, *circa 1940s, $4-6.*

Old Main Building, University of Arizona. Architect C.H. Creighton completed the building in 1891; it was originally intended to be the School of Mines. Sandoval News Co., *circa 1930s, $5-7.*

Women's Dormitories, Yuma and Maricopa Halls, University of Arizona. C.T. Art Colortone, *circa 1940s, $4-6.*

Chapter Ten:

Yuma and the Territorial Prison

Yuma is located along the confluence of the Colorado River, which is the longest river in the West, and the Gila River. Long before the Spanish would "discover" and map the area that became the Yuma Crossing, native peoples such as the Yuman, Quechan, and Cocopah had inhabited the area. Hernando de Alarcon, a Spanish conquistador, navigated the Colorado River with his fleet of three ships, and Alarcon helped Coronado with a land expedition through the area in 1540. Padre Eusebio Kino visited the area several times and is credited with being the first person to map the area. While Kino and other missionaries would establish Catholic missions, there would be years of unrest and uprisings before the area would become settled. When the U.S. acquired the area from Mexico, through the Treaty of Guadalupe Hidalgo in 1848, the boundary with California was set at the southern bank of the Colorado River.

The California gold rush in 1849 created a demand for a ferry that would allow safe crossing across the Colorado River into California. When a system of pulling a large raft was established, it's possible that as many as 60,000 immigrants, who hoped to strike it rich in the California gold fields, traveled across during a two-year period at the price of $2 each. Ft. Yuma was built in 1852. In 1854, Colonel Charles Poston reached the crossing, along with a group that included several engineers; one of those engineers was Herman Ehrenberg, who had been exploring for minerals in Southern Arizona. Several different stories exist about how Charles Poston, in an effort to raise money for their crossing, is credited with surveying and laying out the town of Colorado City, which would eventually be renamed Yuma in 1875. Poston would later be called "The Father of Arizona" for his efforts to have the United States Congress recognize Arizona as a separate territory. Charles Poston foresaw the potential of constructing a bridge across the Colorado River for the projected continental railroad and the importance of navigation on the Colorado River. When the Southern Pacific Railroad arrived in Yuma in 1877, there were about sixteen steamboats operating on the Colorado River, but by 1916 few of the steamboats were still operating. By 1884, Yuma had sanitariums to treat consumptives; mining and ranching contributed to the development of Yuma; and, after a system of irrigation canals was developed, farmers were able to grow alfalfa, melons, citrus, cotton, dates, lettuce, pecans, and wheat. Agriculture and mining are still important to Yuma's economy. Recreation along the Colorado River and retirement RV Parks and housing developments also contribute to Yuma's economy.

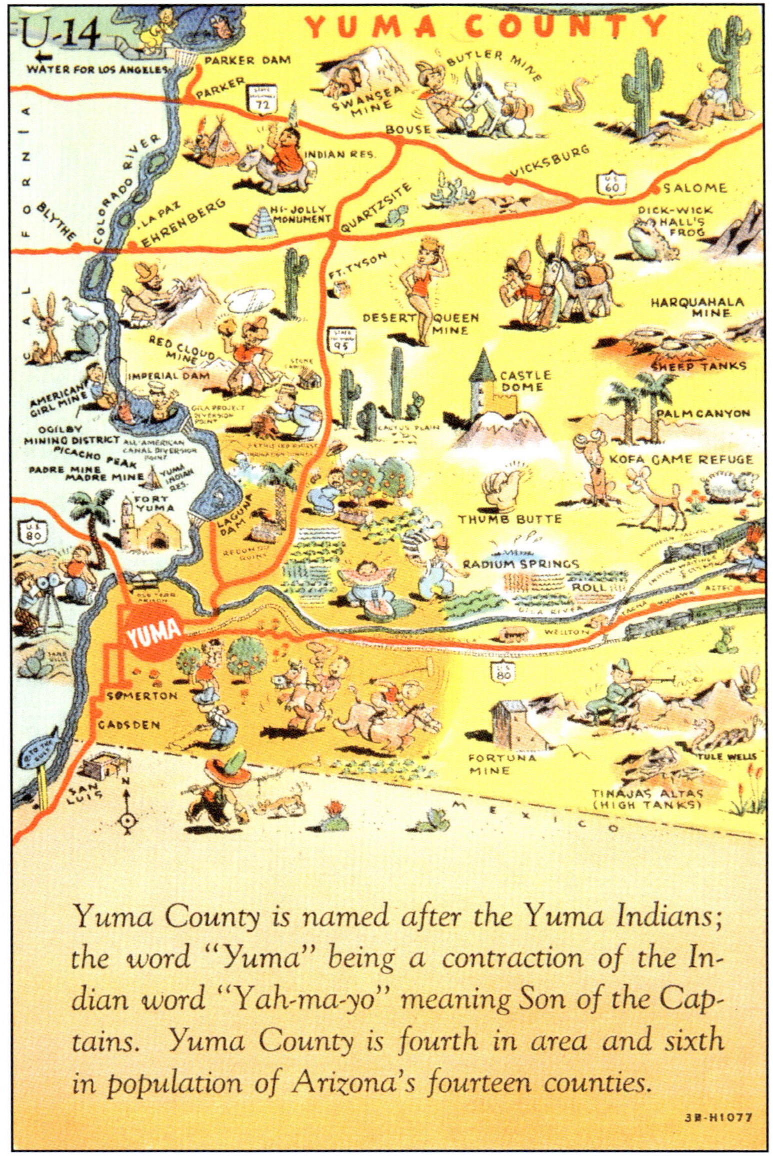

Greetings from Yuma, Arizona. The city boasts a year-around agricultural center. Yuma County is named after the Yuma Indians. C.T. Art Colortone, *circa 1940s, $7-9.*

Greetings from Yuma, Arizona. The city boasts a year-around agricultural center. Yuma County is named after the Yuma Indians. C.T. Art Colortone, *circa 1940s, $7-9.*

Colorado River, Yuma Arizona, Souvenir Publishing Co. *Circa 1917, $7-9.*

Indians Selling Bead Work, Yuma, Arizona. Newman Post Card Co., *circa 1920s, $8-10.*

Southern Pacific Railroad Iron Bridge over the Colorado River, Yuma, Arizona. Newman Post Card Co., *circa 1920, $7-9.*

Colorado River, Yuma, Arizona. Bridges along the Colorado River separate Arizona from California. Newman Post Card Co., *circa 1920, $7-9.*

Southern Pacific Railroad Depot, Yuma, Arizona. *Circa 1930, $7-9.*

Looking North on Main Street, Yuma, Arizona. C.T. Art Colortone, *circa 1954, $4-6.*

Typical Southern Sidewalk Colonnades, Main Street, Yuma, Arizona. C.T. Art Colortone, *circa 1940s, $4-6.*

Cupid's Corner Wedding Chapel, Yuma, Arizona. Real Picture Postcard, *circa 1949, $10-15.*

East Entrance, Yuma, Arizona. Real Picture Postcard, *circa 1950, $12-15.*

Courthouse, Yuma, Arizona. Yuma's second County Courthouse was built in 1928. C.T. Art Colortone, *circa 1940s, $5-7.*

Hotel San Carlos, Yuma, Arizona. The beautiful, four-story art deco hotel was built in 1940. C.T. Art Colortone, *circa 1949, $7-9.*

Yuma Union High School, Yuma, Arizona.
Circa 1940, $7-9.

Gretna Green Wedding Chapel, Yuma, Arizona. MWM, color litho, *circa 1958, $7-9.*

Railway Club, Yuma, Arizona. *Circa 1930s, $7-9.*

Hotel Del Sol, Yuma, Arizona.
Formerly the Hotel del Ming, it was built in 1927.
Hertz Post Cards, *circa 1949, $8-10.*

Post Office, Yuma, Arizona.
C.T. Art Colortone, *1954, $5-7.*

Crossing the American Sahara near Yuma, Arizona.
C.T. American Art Colored,
circa 1930s, $4-6.

The Prison

The Yuma Territorial Prison, nicknamed the "Hell Hole," opened in Yuma on July 1, 1876 with seven prisoners who had been forced to construct their own adobe cells. The Arizona Territorial Legislature had allotted $25,000 for the prison, which was located high on a ridge above the Gila and Colorado Rivers. Escape was almost impossible due to the rivers and desert, with little more than sand and rocks for miles beyond Yuma. There were so few places that would have provided any relief from the blazing sun, and temperatures during the summer months often reached over 120 degrees. While stories exist about supposed escapes from the Yuma Territorial Prison, none have been documented. During the time the prison was in operation, it served twenty-nine female and 3,040 male prisoners who had been convicted of murders, robberies, cattle rustling, and polygamy. Those who broke the prison rules were confined in solitary in a pit known as the "Snake Den." The "Snake Den" was a ten-by-ten space blasted into the rock where a prisoner faced total darkness without a bunk, blanket, or toilet facilities. Prisoners told stories of receiving scorpion and other bites while in the "Snake Pit." Cooperative prisoners were given productive jobs; however, troublemakers often faced long hours in the sun making adobe bricks or breaking rocks. By 1909, a new prison had been built in Florence, Arizona and the last prisoner was transferred. Over time the prison had a variety of uses, but today the Arizona State Parks Association runs the prison and a number of interesting photos of the prisoners and artifacts are on display in the museum.

Portion of Ruins of the Old Territorial Prison, Yuma, Arizona.
C.T. Art Colortone, *circa 1940s, $4-6.*

Territorial Prison Museum on Prison Hill, Yuma, Arizona.
C.T. Art Colortone, *circa 1940s, $4-6.*

Tank Station, Arizona Territorial Prison, Yuma, Arizona.
Real Picture Postcard, *circa 1951, $7-9.*

Arizona Territorial Prison, nicknamed the "Hell Hole," Yuma, Arizona.
Real Picture Postcard, *circa 1950, $7-9.*

Historical Old Prison, Yuma, Arizona.
Real Picture Postcard, Frasher's Fotos, *circa 1949, $7-9.*

Bibliography

Alcock, John. *Sonoran Desert Spring*. Chicago and London: University of Chicago Press, 1985.

Clark, Victoria. *How Arizona Sold Its Sunshine, Historical Hotels of Arizona*. Sedona, Arizona: Blue Gourd Publishing, 2004.

Cooper, Evelyn S. *Arizona's Hal Empie, His Life, His Times, and His Art*. Tempe, Arizona: Arizona Historical Foundation, Arizona State University, 2001.

Dreyfuss, John J. Editor. *A History of Arizona's Counties and Courthouses*. Tucson, Arizona: The National Society of the Colonial Dames of America in the Sate of Arizona under the Auspices of the Arizona Historical Society, 1972.

Engelbrecht, Lloyd and June-Marie. *Henry C. Trost, Architect of the Southwest*. El Paso, Texas: El Paso Library Association, 1981.

Martin, Douglas. *The Lamp in the Desert, The Story of the University of Arizona*. Tucson, Arizona: University of Arizona Press, 1960.

Miller, Joseph. *Arizona, The Grand Canyon State, A State Guide*. Fourth Revised Edition. New York, New York: Hastings House, 1966.

Olin, George. *House in the Sun, A Natural History of the Sonoran Desert*. Second edition. Tucson, Arizona: Southwest Parks and Monuments Association, 1994.

Schwantes, Carlos A. *Bisbee, Urban Outpost on the Frontier*. Tucson, Arizona: University of Arizona Press, 1992.

Sheridan, Thomas. *Arizona, A History*. Tucson, Arizona: University of Arizona Press, 1995.

Shields, Floyd. *Romance & Sex Life of the Date, A History, Cookbook, and Catalog*. Indio, California: Shields Date Garden, 2007.

Smith, Dean. *Best of Reg*. Phoenix, Arizona: *The Arizona Republic*, 1980.

Trimble, Marshall. *Roadside History of Arizona*. Missoula, Montana: Mountain Press Publishing Company, 1986.

Wagoner, Jay J. *Early Arizona Prehistory to Civil War*. Tucson, Arizona: University of Arizona Press, 1975.

Index